COLOR
SHIFT
BY KNIT PICKS

Photography by Amy Cave

Printed in the United States of America

First Printing, 2017

ISBN 978-1-62767-176-7

Versa Press, Inc
800-447-7829

www.versapress.com

CONTENTS

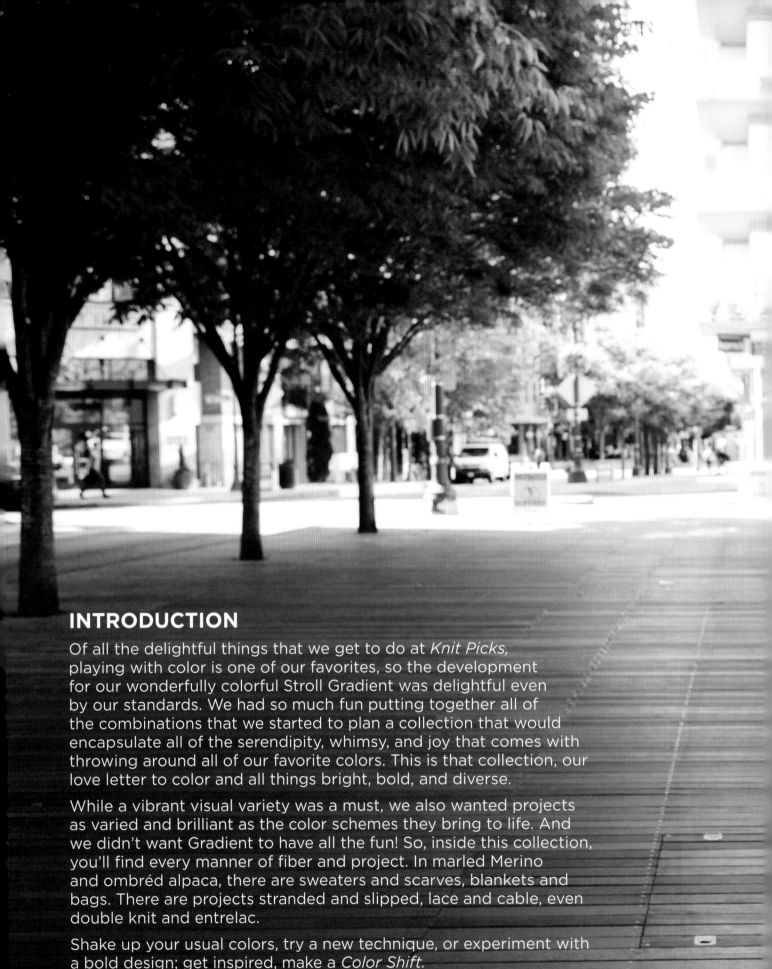

INTRODUCTION

Of all the delightful things that we get to do at *Knit Picks,* playing with color is one of our favorites, so the development for our wonderfully colorful Stroll Gradient was delightful even by our standards. We had so much fun putting together all of the combinations that we started to plan a collection that would encapsulate all of the serendipity, whimsy, and joy that comes with throwing around all of our favorite colors. This is that collection, our love letter to color and all things bright, bold, and diverse.

While a vibrant visual variety was a must, we also wanted projects as varied and brilliant as the color schemes they bring to life. And we didn't want Gradient to have all the fun! So, inside this collection, you'll find every manner of fiber and project. In marled Merino and ombréd alpaca, there are sweaters and scarves, blankets and bags. There are projects stranded and slipped, lace and cable, even double knit and entrelac.

Shake up your usual colors, try a new technique, or experiment with a bold design; get inspired, make a *Color Shift.*

MOTLEY ENTRELAC BLANKET

by Holli Yeoh

FINISHED MEASUREMENTS

44.5 x 59"

YARN

Knit Picks Chroma Twist Bulky (70% Superwash Wool, 30% Nylon; 127 yards/100g): MC Lupine 27288, 10 skeins; C1 Get Your Neon 27291, 9 skeins

NEEDLES

US 10 (6mm) 32" or longer circular needle plus DPNs, or size to obtain gauge

NOTIONS

Stitch Markers
Size J-10 (6mm) Crochet Hook
Smooth Waste Yarn
Yarn Needle

GAUGE

14 sts and 20 rows = 4" in Stockinette stitch, blocked

Motley Entrelac Blanket

Notes:

Cozy up under bold blocks of color. Two colors alternate for each tier of triangles and diamonds in this entrelac blanket. Applied I-cord is worked around the perimeter using the live sts from the provisional cast on and at the top of the blanket and by picking up sts along the selvedges.

Due to the short rows in this project, instead of turning and purling you might consider knitting backwards with the RS facing. This might change your tension somewhat because many knitters have a different tension for their knit and purl sts. Be sure to work your gauge swatch in the same manner.

Provisional Crochet Cast On

With waste yarn, make a slip knot and insert crochet hook. Holding hook in right hand and knitting needle in the other, *bring working yarn behind needle and with hook, reach over top of needle and crochet a chain st thus wrapping yarn around needle; rep from * until desired number of sts are cast on. Work a few more chain sts (not around knitting needle) and fasten off.

Plain I-cord (worked over 5 sts, using two DPNs)

*K5, without turning work, slide sts to opposite end of needle to work next row from RS, pull yarn tightly from the end of the row; rep from *.

DIRECTIONS

With waste yarn and using Provisional Crochet Cast On method, CO 108 sts. With C1, *P18 sts, PM; rep from * 4 times more, P18 sts. 5 markers.

Base Triangle

*Row 1 (RS): K2; turn.

Row 2 (WS): P2; turn.

Row 3: K3; turn.

Row 4 and all WS rows: Purl to end; turn.

Row 5: K4; turn.

Rep last 2 rows working to marker, adding one more st at end of every RS row. 18 sts in Base Triangle, ending with a RS row; do not turn.

Rep from * to end of CO row (removing markers), end last triangle with a RS row. 6 Base Triangles. Break C1.

Left Triangle

Join MC.

Row 1 (WS): P2; turn.

Row 2 (RS): K1, M1, K1.

Row 3: P2, P2TOG; turn.

Row 4: Knit to last st, M1, K1. 1 st inc.

Rep last 2 rows working one more purl st every WS row until all sts along adjacent diamond have been worked, end with a WS row; do not turn. 18 sts in triangle.

First Tier Diamonds

With WS facing, PU and P18 evenly along side of next triangle/diamond; turn.

Row 1 and all RS rows: K18; turn.

Row 2 (WS): P17, P2TOG; turn.

Rep last 2 rows until all sts along adjacent triangle/diamond have been worked, end with a WS row; do not turn. One diamond is complete.

Work 4 more First Tier Diamonds.

Right Triangle

With WS facing, PU and P18 sts evenly along side of next triangle/diamond.

Row 1 (RS): K1, K2TOG, K15; turn. 1 st dec.

Row 2 (WS): Purl to end.

Rep last 2 rows working one fewer knit sts every RS row until 2 sts remain, ending with a WS row. Break MC. With C1 K2TOG; do not turn. 1 st remains in Right Triangle.

Second Tier Diamonds

With RS facing, PU and K17 sts evenly along side of next triangle/diamond; turn. 18 sts including last st of Right Triangle.

Row 1 (WS): P18; turn.

Row 2 (RS): K17, SSK; turn.

Rep last 2 rows until all sts on adjacent diamond/triangle have been worked, end with a RS row; do not turn. One diamond is complete.

Work 5 more Second Tier Diamonds, picking up 1 extra st to replace final Right Triangle st for all diamonds. Break C1.

**Work 1 Left Triangle.

Work 5 First Tier Diamonds.

Work 1 Right Triangle.

Work 6 Second Tier Diamonds.

Rep from ** 5 times more.

Work 1 Left Triangle.

Work 5 First Tier Diamonds.

Work 1 Right Triangle.

End Triangles

With RS facing and C1, PU and K17 sts evenly along side of next triangle/diamond; turn. 18 sts including last st of Right Triangle.

Row 1 (WS): P18; turn.

Row 2 (RS): K17, SSK; turn.

Row 3: P17; W&T.

Row 4: K16, SSK; turn.

Rep last 2 rows, working 1 fewer knit sts every RS row, until all sts on adjacent diamond/triangle have been worked, end with a RS row. 18 sts (17 wrapped sts plus last st).

Work 5 more End Triangles, picking up 1 extra st to replace final Right Triangle st for all triangles. 108 sts. Break C1.

Finishing

I-cord edging is worked from WS so it will curl towards the RS, creating a frame for the blanket.

With WS facing, and MC, CO 5 sts on end of left needle. Work applied I-cord as follows. (it's not necessary to pick up wraps from the short rows.)

Row 1: K1 TBL, K3, K2TOG TBL, with left needle, PU 1 st from edge, transfer sts from right needle to left needle.

Row 2: K1 TBL, K3, K2TOG TBL, transfer sts from right needle to left needle.

Rep last 2 rows until all End Triangles are worked.

To turn corner, work 3 rows of Plain I-cord with 2 DPNs.

PU and K1 from selvedge. Work applied I-cord with 2 DPNs as follows:

Next Row: *K1 TBL, K3, K2TOG TBL, PU and K1, slide sts to opposite end of needle; rep from * into each row to next corner.
At corner, work 3 rows of Plain I-cord.
Carefully remove provisional cast on and transfer sts to circular needle.
Work applied I-cord with circular needle as for other end.
At corner, work 3 rows of Plain I-cord.
Work applied I-cord as for other selvedge.
Graft end of I-cord to beginning of I-cord.

Weave in ends.
Wash and Block to measurements.

GRADIENT PULLOVER

by Alice Tang

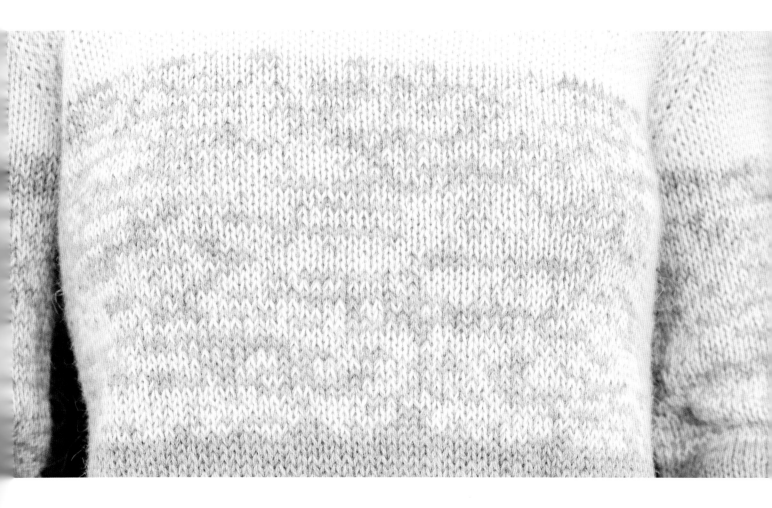

FINISHED MEASUREMENTS.
33.75 (38.25, 41.75, 46.25, 59.75)" bust circumference

YARN
Knit Picks Alpaca Cloud Fingering (100% Superfine Alpaca; 200 yards/50g): C1 Anna 26877, 7 (8, 9, 10, 10) skeins; C2 Sophia 26912, 6 (6, 7, 8, 8) skeins

NEEDLES
US 8 (5mm) straight or circular needles plus DPNs, or size to obtain gauge

NOTIONS
Yarn Needle
Stitch Holder

GAUGE
18 sts and 26 rows = 4" in St st with yarn held double, blocked

Gradient Pullover

Notes:

The pullover has a straight body and set in sleeves with a crew neck. The front and back are worked flat from bottom up.

The pullover uses two strands of each color separately and one strand of each color to achieve a gradient of three colors by using mixed colors.

K1, P1 Ribbing (worked flat or in the rnd over multiples of 2 sts)
All Rows/Rnds: (K1, P1) rep to end.

DIRECTIONS

Back

The Back is worked flat, from the hem up.
Loosely CO 76 (86, 94, 104, 112) sts, using 2 strands of color C1.
Work K1, P1 Ribbing for 2".

WE in St st until 11.5" from cast on, or 6.5" less than desired length from hem to underarm (check your favorite pullover sweater for length, this varies greatly based on back waist length and personal preference.)

Start working with 1 strand of C1 and 1 strand of C2. WE for 6.5".

Shape Armhole

Change to 2 strands of color C2 yarn.
BO 4 (5, 6, 7, 8) sts at beginning of next 2 rows. 68 (76, 82, 90, 96) sts.
BO 1 st at both ends EOR 4 (5, 6, 7, 8) times. 60 (66, 70, 76, 80) sts.
BO 1 st at both ends every 4th row 1 (2, 2, 2, 2) times. 58 (62, 66, 72, 76) sts.
WE until armholes are 7.25 (7.5, 8, 8.25, 8.5)" long.

Shape Shoulder

BO 8 (8, 9, 9, 9) sts at beginning of next 2 rows. 42 (46, 48, 54, 58) sts.
BO 8 (9, 9, 10, 10) sts at beginning of next 2 rows. Put remaining 26 (28, 30, 34, 38) sts on stitch holder.

Front

Work same as Back until armhole length is 5 (4.75, 5.25, 5.25, 5.25)". 58 (62, 66, 72, 76) sts.

Shape Neck

Work 23 (25, 26, 28, 29) sts, put next 12 (12, 14, **16**, 18) sts on holder, add another end of yarn (2 strands of C2) work other side of neck's 23 (25, 26, 28, 29) sts.
Next 2 Rows: BO 2 sts at the beginning of each neck edge. 21 (23, 24, 26, 27) sts each side of neck.
BO 1 st at neck edge EOR 5 (6, 6, 7, 8) times. 16 (17, 18, 19, 19) sts each side of neck.

WE until armholes are 7.25 (7.5, 8, 8.25, 8.5)" long.

Shape Shoulders

BO 8 (8, 9, 9, 9) sts at shoulder edge of next 2 rows. 8 (9, 9, 10, 10) sts at each shoulder.
BO all sts.

Sleeves

The sleeves are worked flat from the wrists up.
CO 40 (43, 45, 47, 50) with 2 strands of C1.
Work K1, P1 Ribbing for 2".
Work in St st for 13.5", or 6.5" less than desired sleeve length, then change yarn to 1 strand C1 and 1 strand C2. At the same time, Inc 1 st at each end of the row, every 6 (6, 6, 5, 5) rows 8 (9, 10, 11, 13) times. 56 (61, 65, 69, 76) sts.

Continue to WE until 20" from CO, or desired sleeve length. Change to 2 strands of C2 yarn.

Shape Sleeve Cap

BO 4 (5, 6, 7, 8) sts at beginning of next 2 rows. 48 (51, 53, 55, 60) sts.

Dec Row: BO 1 st at beginning and end of row. 2 sts dec.
Work a Dec Row EOR a total of 13 (14, 13, 14, 17) times. 22 (23, 27, 27, 26) sts.
Work a Dec Row every 4th row 2 (2, 3, 3, 2) times. 18 (19, 21, 21, 22) sts.
Dec 4 (4, 5, 5, 5) st at beginning of next 2 rows. 10 (11, 11, 11, 12) sts.

BO all sts.

Finishing

Sew shoulder seams.

Neck Band

Work the neck band in K1, P1 Ribbing in the rnd.
With RS facing and DPN's, work 26 (28, 30, 34, 38) back neck sts from holder, PU 16 (17, 18, 18, 19) sts from front neck side, work 12 (12, 14, **16**, 18) front neck sts from holder, PU 16 (17, 18, 18, 19) sts from other neck side. PM for beginning of rnd. 70 (74, 80, **86**, 94) sts.
Work 1", BO loosely.

Sew side seams, sew sleeve seams, sew sleeve to body.
Weave in ends and block.

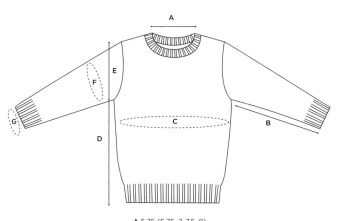

A 5.75 (5.75, 7, 7.5, 8)
B 20 (20, 20, 20, 20)
C 34 (38, 42, 46, 50)
D 18 (18, 18, 18, 18)
E 7.25 (7.5, 8, 8.25, 8.5)
F 12.5 (13.5, 14.5, 15.5, 17)
G 8.75 (9.5, 10, 10.5, 11)

CONCENTRICAL COWL

by Stana D. Sortor

FINISHED MEASUREMENTS
Cowl (Scarf): 7" high x 25.75 (46)" circumference

YARN
Knit Picks Chroma Fingering (70% Superwash Wool, 30% Nylon; 396 yards/100g): MC Natural 25248, 1(2) skeins; C1 Pegasus 26546, 1 skein

NEEDLES
US 3 (3.25mm) DPNs or two 24" circular needles for two circulars technique, or one 32" or longer circular needle for Magic Loop technique, or size to obtain gauge

NOTIONS
Yarn Needle
Stitch Markers
Crochet Hook and Scrap Yarn (or as preferred for Provisional CO)
Stitch Holder, or spare circular needle and DPNs

GAUGE
30 sts and 34 rows = 4" in stranded St st in the round, blocked

Concentrical Cowl

Notes:

This infinity cowl or scarf is knit in the round. The Fair Isle stranded colorwork pattern is repeated nine times for cowl and 16 times for scarf, with an added stripe in a natural color. The provisional cast on is joined to the opposite end with Kitchener Stitch technique for a truly invisible join and infinity loop appeal. The chart is followed from bottom to top, working each row from right to left and knitting all stitches, four times across the round.

Kitchener Stitch (grafting)

With an equal number of sts on two needles, thread end through yarn needle. Hold needles parallel, with WS's facing in and both needles pointing to the right.

Perform Step 2 on the first front st, and then Step 4 on the first back st, and then continue with instructions below.

1: Pull yarn needle K-wise through front st and drop st from knitting needle.

2: Pull yarn needle P-wise through next front st, leave st on knitting needle.

3: Pull yarn needle P-wise through first back st and drop st from knitting needle.

4: Pull yarn needle K-wise through next back st, leave st on knitting needle.

Repeat Steps 1 – 4 until all sts have been grafted.

Gradient Infinity Pattern, Written Directions (worked in the rnd over multiples of 26 sts)

Rnd 1: K1 in MC, K1 in C1, K3 in MC, K3 in C1, (K3 in MC, K1 in C1) 2x, K3 in MC, K3 in C1, K3 in MC, K1 in C1.

Rnd 2: K2 in MC, K1 in C1, K3 in MC, K3 in C1, K3 in MC, K1 in C1, K1 in MC, K1 in C1, K3 in MC, K3 in C1, K3 in MC, K1 in C1, K1 in MC.

Rnd 3: (K3 in MC, K1 in C1, K3 in MC, K3 in C1) 2x, K3 in MC, K1 in C1, K2 in MC.

Rnd 4: (K1 in C1, K3 in MC) 2x, K3 in C1, K5 in MC, K3 in C1, K3 in MC, K1 in C1, K3 in MC.

Rnd 5: K2 in C1, K3 in MC, K1 in C1, (K3 in MC, K3 in C1) 2x, (K3 in MC, K1 in C1) 2x.

Rnd 6: K3 in C1, K3 in MC, K1 in C1, K3 in MC, K3 in C1, K1 in MC, K3 in C1, K3 in MC, K1 in C1, K3 in MC, K2 in C1.

Rnd 7: K1 in MC, K3 in C1, K3 in MC, K1 in C1, K3 in MC, K5 in C1, K3 in MC, K1 in C1, K3 in MC, K3 in C1.

Rnd 8: K2 in MC, (K3 in C1, K3 in MC, K1 in C1, K3 in MC) 2x, K3 in C1, K1 in MC.

Rnd 9: K3 in MC, K3 in C1, (K3 in MC, K1 in C1) 3x, K3 in MC, K3 in C1, K2 in MC.

Rnd 10: K1 in C1, K3 in MC, K3 in C1, K3 in MC, K1 in C1, K5 in MC, K1 in C1, K3 in MC, K3 in C1, K3 in MC.

Rnd 11: K1 in MC, K1 in C1, K3 in MC, K3 in C1, (K3 in MC, K1 in C1) 2x, K3 in MC, K3 in C1, K3 in MC, K1 in C1.

Rnd 12: K2 in MC, K1 in C1, K3 in MC, K3 in C1, K3 in MC, K1 in C1, K1 in MC, K1 in C1, K3 in MC, K3 in C1, K3 in MC, K1 in C1, K1 in MC.

Rnd 13: Rep Rnd 11.

Rnd 14: Rep Rnd 10.

Rnd 15: Rep Rnd 9.

Rnd 16: Rep Rnd 8.

Rnd 17: Rep Rnd 7.

Rnd 18: Rep Rnd 6.

Rnd 19: Rep Rnd 5.

Rnd 20: Rep Rnd 4.

Rnd 21: Rep Rnd 3.

Rnd 22: Rep Rnd 2.

Rnd 23: Rep Rnd 1.

Rep Rnds 1-23 for pattern, or as directed.

DIRECTIONS

Using the provisional cast on technique of your choice, CO 104 sts onto scrap yarn. Attach MC. Being careful not to twist the sts, PM at the first st and begin to knit in the round.

Rnds 1-7: Knit in MC. After final rnd, attach C1.

Rnds 8-30: Work Gradient Infinity Pattern Rnds 1-23, repeating row four times across the rnd, using either Gradient Infinity Chart or line-by-line instructions.

Rnds 31-206 (31-360): Repeat the Gradient Infinity Pattern Rnds 2-23 eight (15) times. After final rnd, cut C1.

Rounds 207-218 (361-392): Knit in MC. Cut yarn, leaving a tail at least three time the length of the sts.

Join Ends:

Remove the scrap yarn from the provisionally cast on sts and place the resulting live stitches on a spare needle. Join together these cast on sts with the live sts already on the needles, using yarn tail and Kitchener Stitch technique for an invisible seam.

Finishing

Weave in ends, wash and block to finished measurements.

Concentrical Cowl

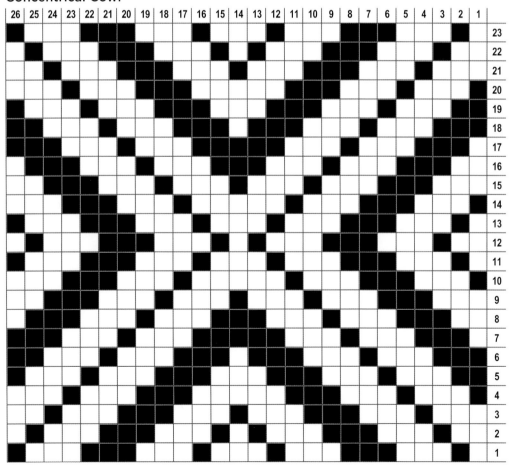

| 26 | 25 | 24 | 23 | 22 | 21 | 20 | 19 | 18 | 17 | 16 | 15 | 14 | 13 | 12 | 11 | 10 | 9 | 8 | 7 | 6 | 5 | 4 | 3 | 2 | 1 | |

Rows: 23, 22, 21, 20, 19, 18, 17, 16, 15, 14, 13, 12, 11, 10, 9, 8, 7, 6, 5, 4, 3, 2, 1

Legend:

☐	**knit** knit stitch
☐	MC
■	CC

BARNSDALL CARDI

by Laura Birek

FINISHED MEASUREMENTS

32.75 (35.75, 40, 44.25, 48.25, 52.5, 56.75, 61)" finished bust measurement, buttoned; garment is meant to be worn with 0" of ease

YARN

Knit Picks Stroll Sock Yarn (75% Superwash Merino Wool, 25% Nylon; 231 yards/50g): MC White 26082, 4 (4, 5, 5, 6, 6, 7, 7) balls

Knit Picks Stroll Gradient (75% Superwash Merino Wool, 25% Nylon; 458 yards/100g): C1 Sea You Later 27390, 3 (3, 3, 3, 3, 4, 4, 4) skein. Yarn requirements are written to match stripes properly, with no breaks in the color gradient pattern. If knitting with a solid color C1, 150 (150, 150, 200, 200, 250, 250, 250)g of yarn required

NEEDLES

US 6 (4mm) circular needles at least 32 (32, 32, 40, 40, 40, 47, 47)" long, plus DPNs or two 24" circular needles for two circulars technique, or one 32" or longer circular needle for Magic Loop technique, or size to obtain gauge

US 4 (3.5mm) circular needles at least 32 (32, 40, 40, 40, 40, 40, 40)" long, plus DPNs or two 24" circular needles for two circulars technique, or one 32" or longer circular needle for Magic Loop technique, or size to obtain gauge

NOTIONS

Yarn Needle
Stitch Markers
2 flexible Stitch Holders or Scrap Yarn
7 7/8" or 1" Buttons

GAUGE

21 sts and 31 rows = 4" in St st worked flat and in the rnd on larger needles, blocked
21 sts and 42 rows = 4" in Garter st worked flat on smaller needles, blocked

Barnsdall Cardi

Notes:

The body and sleeves of this pattern are knit seamlessly from the top down in Stockinette stitch, with the armhole stitches held while you work the body. The button band is picked up around the entire front width in one piece, and worked in Garter stitch for 1.5". Ideally, you will match your arm stripes to the body by starting a new ball of the gradient yarn at the same point in the colorway as the held stitches. The best way to do this is to weigh your C1 yarn before casting on, and then again after you've placed the armhole sts on holders. Then, take a new ball of C1 and wind off the difference, and start each armhole at that point in the colorway. For example, if you have a 100g ball before casting on, and 85g after you've knit to the armhole split, you have used 15g of C1 so far, and would wind off 15g of C1 from a new ball before starting each armhole. If you don't have a reliable scale, you can just eyeball the amount and take care to make sure the stripe colors match up at the join.

Sizes 40" and above will likely need to begin a second ball of C1 while knitting the main body, and sizes 52.5" and above may have to start a second ball for each sleeve. To match stripes when you've come to the end of a ball, begin knitting from the opposite end on the new ball. For example, if you knit the first part of the sweater by pulling from the center of the ball, join the second ball by pulling from the outside instead. This will allow your colors to transition seamlessly.

The button band is worked in one piece, with seven 2-stitch buttonholes placed evenly. I have written the pattern to use a two-row buttonhole, but you can use whichever buttonhole technique you prefer.

The arms are knit in the round using DPNs, or two circulars technique, or Magic Loop technique. The cuffs and bottom hem are knit in a K2, P2 Rib using the smaller needle size.

All color change rows start on a WS row when working flat. This allows the M1 increases to use the same color as the base stitch, blending the increases better and keeping the stripe pattern smooth. Note that each row shown on the chart is worked twice.

2x2 Rib (worked flat or in the rnd over multiples of 4 sts)
All Rows/Rnds: *K2, P2; rep from * to end.

Stripe Pattern (worked flat or in the rnd in St st, starting with a WS row)
Rows 1-4: MC.
Rows 5-6: C1.
Rows 7-8: MC.
Rows 9-10: C1.
Rows 11-14: MC.
Rows 15-18: C1.
Rows 19-20: MC.
Rows 21-32: Rep Rows 7-18.
Rep Rows 1-32 for pattern.

DIRECTIONS

Yoke

With larger needle and MC, loosely CO 54 (60, 66, 72, 78, 84, 90, 96) sts.

Set-up Row (WS): P5 (6, 7, 8, 9, 10, 11, 12) sts, PM, P11 (12, 13, 14, 15, 16, 17, 18), PM, P22 (24, 26, 28, 30, 32, 34, 36) sts, PM, P11 (12, 13, 14, 15, 16, 17, 18) sts, PM, P5 (6, 7, 8, 9, 10, 11, 12) sts to end of row.

Yoke Increase Row (RS): K2, M1, *K to 1 st before M, M1, K1, SM, K1, M1: rep from * 3 more times, K to 2 sts before end of row, M1, K2. 10 sts inc. 64 (70, 76, 82, 88, 94, 100, 106) sts.
P across.
Begin working Stripe Pattern, starting at Row 4.
Rep Yoke Increase Row every RS row 21 (23, 26, 29, 32, 35, 38, 41) more times while working Stripe Pattern, until you have 274 (300, 336, 372, 408, 444, 480, 516) sts. Make note of the row you're on in the Stripe Pattern, you will need to start at this same row when picking up the sleeves later.

Join Body and Hold Sleeves

You will now knit across the body of the sweater, placing the active sleeve sts on a holder or on scrap yarn in a contrasting color. K49 (54, 61, 68, 75, 82, 89, 96) sts to M, SM, place next 55 (60, 67, 74, 81, 88, 95, 102) sts on holder, remove M, K66 (72, 80, 88, 96, 104, 112, 120) Back sts to M, SM, place next 55 (60, 67, 74, 81, 88, 95, 102) sts on holder, remove M, K49 (54, 61, 68, 75, 82, 89, 96) sts to end. 164 (180, 202, 224, 246, 268, 290, 312) sts remain on needles.

Waist Decreases

Continuing in Stripe Pattern, begin waist decreases.
Work even in St st for 5 (1, 1, 3, 1, 1, 1, 5) rows.

Waist Decrease Row: *K to 2 sts before M, SSK, SM, K2tog; rep from *, K to end. 4 sts dec. 160 (176, 198, 220, 242, 264, 286, 308) sts.
Work even in St st for 9 (11, 11, 9, 9, 7, 7, 5) rows.
Rep Waist Decrease Row followed by St st rows 7 (6, 6, 6, 6, 7, 7, 7) times total until 136 (156, 178, 200, 222, 240, 262, 284) sts remain on needles.

Work even in St st for 4 (2, 0, 4, 2, 2, 0, 4) rows.

Hip Increases

Continuing in Stripe Pattern, begin hip increases.
Hip Increase Row: *K to 1 st before M, M1, SM, M1, repeat from * once more, K to end. 4 sts inc. 140 (160, 182, 204, 226, 244, 266, 288) sts.
Work even in St st for 5 rows.
Rep Hip Increase Row followed by St st rows 9 (10, 9, 9, 9, 10, 9, 9) times total. 172 (196, 214, 236, 258, 280, 298, 320) sts.

Sizes 32.75 (35.75, 44.25, 52.5, 61)" only: K across, removing Ms as you go. 172 (196, 236, 280, 320) sts.
Sizes 40 (48.25, 56.75)" only: *K to M, remove M, K2tog, repeat from * once more, K to end of row. 212 (256, 296) sts.

Hem

With smaller circular needles and MC, work in 2x2 Rib for 12 rows. BO all sts loosely in rib.

Sleeves (make 2 the same)

Work one sleeve at a time, being careful to start on the correct row of the Stripe Pattern as noted when you placed the sts on holders, and matching the C1 color as described in the pattern notes. Sleeves are knit in the round, so all rows will be K. Continue the Stripe Pattern until you reach the cuff.

With larger DPNs, or two circulars, or long circular for Magic Loop technique, place 55 (60, 67, 74, 81, 88, 95, 102) sts from holder onto needles.

PU and K 3 sts from underarm gap, then K across held sts. 58 (63, 70, 77, 84, 91, 98, 105) sts. Join rnd at underarm, PM for beginning of rnd, then K to end of rnd.

Work 2 (0, 0, 3, 6, 1, 6, 1) rnds even in St st.

Sleeve Decrease: SSK, K to 2 sts before M, K2tog. 2 sts dec.
Work 10 (9, 7, 6, 5, 5, 4, 4) rnds even in St st.
Repeat Sleeve Decrease followed by St st rnds 13 (15, 19, 21, 24, 26, 29, 32) times total until 32 (33, 32, 35, 36, 39, 40, 41) sts remain.

Cuff

Cuff is knit in MC only. Switch to MC and smaller DPNs.
Sizes 32.75 (40, 48.25, 56.75): K one rnd. 32 (32, 36, 40) sts.
Sizes 35.75 (61): SSK, K to end of rnd. 32 (40) sts.
Size 44.25 (52.5): M1, K to end of rnd. 36 (40) sts.

Work K2, P2 Rib for 12 rnds.
BO loosely in rib.

Collar and Button Band

With MC and smaller circular needles PU sts along button band and collar. Button Band is worked in Garter st (K every row). Starting at bottom right corner with RS facing, PU and K a total of 340 (346, 358, 368, 378, 390, 402, 412) sts evenly as follows: Along front right body from hem to V-neck opening 104 (101, 98, 95, 92, 89, 87, 84) sts; along front right neckline 39 (42, 48, 53, 58, 64, 69, 74) sts; along CO edge around collar 54 (60, 66, 72, 78, 84, 90, 96) sts; along front left neckline 39 (42, 48, 53, 58, 64, 69, 74) sts; along front left body from V-neck opening to hem: 104 (101, 98, 95, 92, 89, 87, 84) sts.
Work even in Garter st for 7 rows, ending with a WS row.
Buttonhole Row (RS): K 6 (9, 6, 9, 6, 9, 7, 10) sts, *BO 2, K 14 (13, 13, 12, 12, 11, 11, 10) sts, rep from * 6 more times, BO 2, PM, K to end of row.
Next Row (WS): K to M, *CO 2, K 14 (13, 13, 12, 12, 11, 11, 10) sts, rep from * 6 more times, CO 2, K to end of row.
K 8 rows even in Garter st.
BO all sts.

Finishing

Weave in ends, using yarn tail to reinforce underarm if a gap appeared at the join. Wash and block to diagram.
Sew buttons evenly on left side of band, matching the buttonhole spacing.

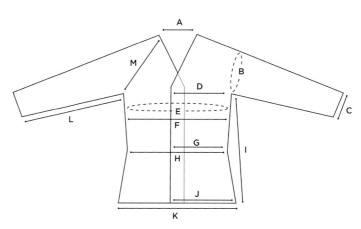

A 4.75 (5.25, 6, 6.5, 7, 7.5, 8.25, 8.75)"
B 11 (12, 13.25, 14.75, 16, 17.25, 18.75, 20)"
C 3 (3, 3.25, 3.5, 3.75, 4, 4)"
D 10 (11, 12.25, 13.75, 15, 16.25, 17.75, 19)"
E 32.75 (35.75, 40, 44.25, 48.25, 52.5, 56.75, 61)"
F 12.75 (13.75, 15.25, 16.75, 18.25, 19.75, 21.26, 22.75)"
G 8.75 (10, 11.25, 12.5, 14, 15, 16.25, 17.75)"
H 10 (11.25, 13, 14.5, 15.75, 17.25, 19, 20)"
I 18.75 (18.25, 17.75, 17.25, 16.75, 16.25, 15.75, 15.25)"
J 10.5 (11.75, 13, 14.25, 15.5, 17, 18, 19.5)"
K 11.75 (13.75, 14.75, 16.5, 18.25, 19.25, 20.75, 22)"
L 21 (21, 20.75, 21.5, 21.75, 21.75, 21.25, 22)"
M 7.25 (7.75, 8.5, 9.25, 10, 10.75, 11.5, 12.25)"

Barnsdall Stripe

3	2	1	
■	■	■	31-32
■	■	■	29-30
			27-28
			25-26
■	■	■	23-24
			21-22
			19-20
■	■	■	17-18
■	■	■	15-16
			13-14
			11-12
■	■	■	9-10
			7-8
■	■	■	5-6
			3-4
			1-2

Legend:

☐ RS: knit
WS: purl

☐ MC

■ C1

Note that each row shown on the chart is worked twice.

GRADIENCE SHAWL

by Holli Yeoh

FINISHED MEASUREMENTS
64" wingspan x 32" depth

YARN
Knit Picks Stroll Gradient (75% Superwash Merino Wool, 25% Nylon; 458 yards/100g): MC Pet Rock 27372, C1 Lifeguard 27383, 1 skein each

NEEDLES
US 4 (3.5mm) 32" circular needle, or size to obtain gauge

NOTIONS
Stitch Marker
Cable Needle
Digital Scale (optional)
Yarn Needle

GAUGE
22 sts and 37 rows = 4" over lace pattern, blocked

Gradience Shawl

Notes:

Bold lines and angles created by the lace make this shawl a striking accessory for your wardrobe. Each side of the classic triangular shawl is worked with an intuitive and simple lace pattern angled towards a central, minimalist cable motif. The pattern allows you to use the full extent of your yarn, ending with several ridges of garter stitch.

You can get creative with the two balls of gradient yarn. With two balls of the same colorway you can alternate every two rows to create wider sections of color or you can join the balls end to end to match the same color in the middle of the project. One ball will be worked from the inside and the other from the outside, with the shawl beginning and ending with the same color. If using two separate colorways, as in the sample shawl, choose balls that share a common color on the inside or outside of the ball so the join is not noticeable in the color progression.

The slipped st at the beginning of every row is always slipped P-wise with the yarn in front, then the yarn is moved to the back (between the needles) before working the next st, which is always a knit st.

When working the charts, RS rows (odd numbers) are read from right to left, and WS rows (even numbers) from left to right. Work the red outlined repeat boxes once the first time the chart is worked, then increase by 1 repeat each time the chart is worked.

C3F: Sl 2 to CN, hold in front, K1, K2 from CN.
C3B: Sl 1 to CN, hold in back, K2, K1 from CN.
C4F: Sl 2 to CN, hold in front, K2, K2 from CN.
C4B: Sl 2 to CN, hold in back, K2, K2 from CN.

This is a great opportunity to practice crossing cables without a cable needle.

C4F without a cable needle
1. Sl 2 (instead of placing them on CN), K2.
2. Insert left needle into front of slipped sts, pinch base of all 4 sts involved in cable, then slide right needle out of the sts.
3. Reinsert right needle into the 2 sts that are not on left needle.
4. K2 from left needle.

C4B without a cable needle
1. Sl 2 WYIF (instead of placing them on CN), K2.
2. Insert left needle into back of slipped sts, pinch base of all 4 sts involved in cable, then slide right needle out of the sts.
3. Reinsert right needle into the 2 sts that are not on left needle.
4. K2 from left needle.

Chart A
Row 1 (RS): Sl 1, (K2, YO) twice, K1, YO, K2, YO, K3. 15 sts.
Row 2 and every WS row: Sl 1, K2, purl to last 3 sts, K3.
Row 3: Sl 1, K2, YO, K4, YO, K1, YO, K4, YO, K3. 19 sts.
Row 5: Sl 1, K2, YO, C3F, K3, YO, K1, YO, K3, C3B, YO, K3. 23 sts.
Row 7: Sl 1, K2, YO, K8, YO, K1, YO, K8, YO, K3. 27 sts.
Row 9: Sl 1, K2, YO, K5, C3B, K2, YO, K1, YO, K2, C3F, K5, YO, K3. 31 sts.
Row 11: Sl 1, K2, YO, K12, YO, K1, YO, K12, YO, K3. 35 sts.

Row 13: Sl 1, K2, YO, K3, C4F, K4, K2TOG, (YO, K1) 3 times, YO, SSK, K4, C4B, K3, YO, K3. 39 sts.
Row 15: Sl 1, K2, YO, K1, YO, SSK, K8, K2TOG, YO, K3, YO, K1, YO, K3, YO, SSK, K8, K2TOG, YO, K1, YO, K3. 43 sts.
Row 16: Rep Row 2.
Rows 1-16 complete Chart A.

Chart B
Row 1 (RS): Sl 1, K2, YO, K1, [K2, YO, SSK] once, K4, C4B, [K2, K2TOG, YO] once, (K1, YO) twice, K1, [YO, SSK, K2] once, C4F, K4, [K2TOG, YO, K2] once, K1, YO, K3. 4 sts inc, 47 sts.
Row 2 and every WS row: Sl 1, K2, purl to last 3 sts, K3.
Row 3: Sl 1, K2, YO, K1, YO, [SSK, K2, YO] once, SSK, K7, [K1, K2TOG, YO, K1] once, K2, YO, K1, YO, K2, [K1, YO, SSK, K1] once, K7, K2TOG, [YO, K2, K2TOG] once, YO, K1, YO, K3. 4 sts inc, 51 sts.
Row 5: Sl 1, K2, YO, K3, [YO, SSK, K2] once, C4F, K4, [K2TOG, YO, K2] once, K2TOG, (YO, K1) 3 times, YO, SSK, [K2, YO, SSK] once, K4, C4B, [K2, K2TOG, YO] once, K3, YO, K3. 4 sts inc, 55 sts.
Row 7: Sl 1, K2, YO, K1, YO, SSK, K1, [K1, YO, SSK, K1] once, K7, K2TOG, [YO, K2, K2TOG] once, YO, K3, YO, K1, YO, K3, YO, [SSK, K2, YO] once, SSK, K7, [K1, K2TOG, YO, K1] once, K1, K2TOG, YO, K1, YO, K3. 4 sts inc, 59 sts.
Row 8: Rep Row 2.
Rep Rows 1-8 for Chart B, increasing 1 rep for instructions in square brackets (not the parentheses) every 8 rows.

Turkish Cast On
1. Hold both needle tips parallel and pointing to the right, with one above the other and place slip knot on lower needle.
2. Wrap yarn around needles by first winding yarn away from yourself and behind the needles in an upward direction, then towards yourself and down in front of the needles. Count each wrap around the needles as a cast on st, not counting the initial slip knot.
3. Pull the lower needle tip to the right, through the sts until the wraps rest on the cable part of the needle.
4. Ensure the working yarn is wrapped under the cable and held it at the back before beginning the first row in the pattern instructions. There should be the same number of wraps on the upper needle and the lower cable (not including the slip knot).

DIRECTIONS

Garter Stitch Tab
Beginning with lightest colored end of MC and using Turkish Cast On, CO 4 sts.
Knit 1 row.
For now, only one side (4 sts) of the CO will be worked; the remaining side will be held on the cable until needed

Next Row: Sl 1 WYIF, K3.
Repeat last row 6 times; do not turn when last row is completed. Garter st tab is 4 sts wide, has 3 slipped sts along each selvedge edge, and has 4 live sts resting on the cable from the Turkish Cast On (not including the slip knot).
PU and K3 sts into the slipped sts along the selvedge edge, drop the slip knot off the needle, knit the 4 Turkish Cast On sts. 11 sts.

Next Row (WS): Sl 1, K2, purl to last 3 sts, K3.

Begin Chart A

Work Rows 1-16 of Chart A from chart or written instructions. 43 sts.

Begin Chart B

Work Rows 1-8 of Chart B from chart or written instructions. 59 sts.

Work Chart B as established for 172 more rows, ending on WS Row 4. When you run out of MC, join C1 from the end of ball that is the same color as the last sts of MC ball. 403 sts.

Optional: A 7-8% yardage buffer is calculated into the pattern. To use the full amount of your remaining yarn, cont in pattern until you have at least 36 g remaining.

Garter Stitch Edging

Place marker just before center st.

RS Row: Sl 1, K2, YO, knit to marker, YO, SM, K1, YO, knit to last 3 sts, YO, K3. 4 sts inc.

WS Row: Sl 1, knit to end.

Repeat last 2 rows 9 times more. 443 sts.

BO loosely.

Finishing

Weave in ends.

Wash and block to measurements.

Chart A

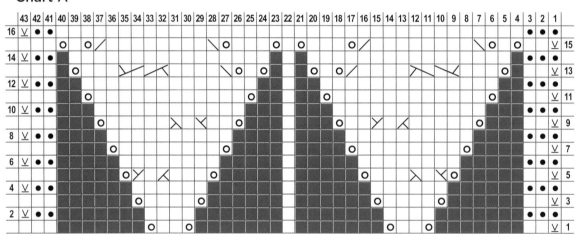

Legend:

- ☐ **knit**
  RS: knit stitch
  WS: purl stitch

- ⊡ **purl**
  RS: purl stitch
  WS: knit stitch

- ■ **no stitch**

- ⊙ **yo**
  Yarn Over

- ⊻ **slip**
  Slip stitch as if to purl,
  holding yarn in front

- ╱ **k2tog**
  Knit two stitches
  together as one stitch

- ╲ **ssk**
  Slip one stitch as if to knit,
  Slip another stitch as if to knit.
  Insert left-hand needle into front
  of these 2 stitches and knit them
  together

- **C3F**
  sl2 to CN, hold in front.
  k1, k2 from CN

- **C3B**
  sl1 to CN, hold in back.
  k2, k1 from CN

- **C4F**
  sl 2 to CN, hold in front.
  k2, k2 from CN

- **C4B**
  sl2 to CN, hold in back.
  k2, k2 from CN

- ☐ **pattern repeat**

Chart B

DANCING CIRCLES REVERSIBLE SCARF

by Magda Stryk Therrien

FINISHED MEASUREMENTS

6" wide x 61" long

YARN

Knit Picks Swish Worsted (100% Superwash Merino Wool; 110 yards/50g): MC Sugar Plum 25142, 1 ball; C1 Amethyst Heather 25147, C2 Indigo Heather 24097, C3 Delft Heather 24095, 2 balls each, C4 Dusk 25150, 1 ball

NEEDLES

US 10 (6mm) straight or circular needles, or size to obtain gauge

NOTIONS

Yarn Needle
Scrap Yarn
Crochet Hook approximately the same size as knitting needle used
Yarn Stranding Guide (optional)

GAUGE

16 sts and 26 rows = 4" over pattern with yarn held double, blocked

Dancing Circles Reversible Scarf

Notes:

This scarf was inspired by Anna Maltz's (SweaterSpotter) marlisle technique. I quickly saw the potential of something else in it and started playing. This scarf is one of the expressions of that something else.

Most of the scarf is simply knit with two different colored strands of yarn held together to make a lovely, squishy garter stitch fabric. The edges are two color I-cord with the yarns interlocked to join them like in any intarsia. The magic comes in the stockinette motifs that pop out of the background in only one of the colors, as opposed to the marled combination. A little bit of double knitting achieves a different colored, solid motif on either side of the fabric.

This is a perfect introduction to both intarsia and double knitting. You will barely realize you are learning new techniques as they are simple and such a tiny part of this piece, you will think of them as just another instruction.

I-cord

Whenever you change yarns along the intarsia I-cord edges, cast on and bind off, bring the new yarn up from underneath the old yarn, interlocking the two strands. It is not necessary to do this for the first pair of sts right after a two-strand stitch as both strands are coming from the same stitch on the previous row, but it is necessary for the second pair of sts so that the sts are connected and you get a smooth I-cord instead of two pairs of unconnected sts. It may be a bit awkward to knit the second pair of sts because the strand of yarn will be loose, but will even up as you knit those two sts.

Any time (like in the cast on or bind off sections) where you are just knitting single strand sts with no two-strand sts, ensure that you intertwine the strands whenever changing colors.

Double Knitting

As you come to each a two-strand st that is being separated for the double knitting (for the circles), you may need to rearrange the strands.

Method 1: This works quite well and any imperfections are lost in the fabric. You can just knit into the color you want to work with. That is, if the color you need is the first strand on the left needle, knit into it as normal. If the color you want to knit into is the second strand, follow the second paragraph in Method 2.

Method 2: If you are a bit of a perfectionist and want to avoid crossing the legs of strands, rearrange them if necessary. Make sure that the strand you want to knit into is the second strand on the left needle. If it is not, slip the second strand over this first, but not off the needle to rearrange into the proper order.

Slip the right needle P-wise into the second strand on the left needle, pinch the sts against the right needle and slip both strands off the left needle. Slip the left needle back into the first strand and slip the second strand back on to the left needle. Now you have rearranged the sts into the proper order with everything oriented the right way. With both yarns at the back, knit the first

st, move both yarns to the front and purl the second st. Once the strands are separated you will always work each color of yarn into a st of the same color.

Refer to the table below to know what you how to work the double knit sts on each side of the scarf.

Working Side	Light Color Circle	Dark Color Circle
Front Side	Knit the light, purl the dark	Knit the dark, purl the light
Back Side	Knit the dark, purl the light	Knit the light, purl the dark

To work the double-knit sts on the front side, *with both yarns behind the left needle, pick up only the color shown on the chart, knit the first strand or st. The color you are knitting with should match the color you are knitting into. Then move both yarns in the front of the needle and purl the second strand or st with the other color (the one not shown on the chart). Move both yarns to the back for the next st. Rep from * for each pair of sts.

When working on the back side, follow the same instructions, but knit with the color not shown on the chart and purl with the color shown.

Be careful not to twist the two yarns in between the knits and purls of the double stitching (in the two-stranded sections, you don't need to pay attention to that). To avoid twisting, keep the yarns separated (you can use a yarn stranding guide or just keep an eye on the yarns) on your finger. On each side, consistently pick up each yarn strand from under or over the other.

When you come to a two-strand knit st above double knitting (with two single strands), you work the new st with both strands into both strands. Work the two double knit strands like an SSK, slip each st K-wise and then knit them together with both strands TBL.

General

The front of the work is easily identified because the visible I-cord sts and the large circles are in the lighter of the two yarns being used together. The larger circles should be the same color as the I-cord edge that is showing on the same side of the scarf, the small circles should be the opposite color.

If you are having trouble figuring out where you are on the chart, first determine whether the you are on the front (larger circles are the lighter color) or the back. Then count the number of garter ridges.

For each pattern repeat, one of the yarns changes and either the old darker color becomes the new lighter color (for repeats 2, 3 and 4) or the old lighter color becomes the new darker color (for repeats 5, 6 and 7).

RS chart rows are read from right to left, and WS rows from left to right. The first 4 stitches and the last 4 stitches on the chart represent the icord edge.

For a video demonstration of how to work Kitchener st, see http://tutorials.knitpicks.com/wptutorials/kitchener-stitch/

How to Videos

There is a series of videos available for this scarf showing various techniques, including the cast on, the I-cord edging, the double knitting from the two-strand sts, and the bind off. These are available at http://www.magdamakes.com/patterns/dancing-circles-scarf.

DIRECTIONS

Cast On

With scrap yarn, crochet 3 chains over your needle. With MC and C1 held together, K 3 sts into the crocheted chain. Sl the sts back to left needle.

Row 1: K1 with both yarns into both strands of the first st, separate the next 2 sts so that the two MC strands are in positions 1 and 2 on the left needle and the two C1 strands are in positions 3 and 4. K2 with MC, bring C1 up from underneath MC and K2 with C1. Sl the 4 single strand sts back to the left needle. There will be 1 two-stranded st remaining on the right needle.

Row 2: M1L with both strands, K2 with MC, K2 with C1 (remembering to intertwine the yarns), Sl the 4 single strand sts back to the left needle. There will be 2 two-strand sts remaining on the right needle.

Row 3: With both strands, knit into the bar between the two-strand st on the right needle and the first st on the left needle (you may have to dig a little to find it), K2 with MC, K2 with C1, Sl the 4 single strand sts back to the left needle. There will be 3 two-strand sts remaining on the right needle.

Rows 4 - 20: Rep Row 3 until there are 20 two-strand sts remaining on the right needle.

Rows 21 - 23: K2 with MC, K2 with C1, Sl the 4 single strand sts back to the left needle.

Move the yarns to the front between the needles. Sl the 4 single strand sts onto the right needle as if purling them together through the back. There are now 20 two-strand sts, the yarn comes to the front, then 2 C1 sts and 2 MC sts on the right needle. Turn.

Row 24: K2 with MC, K2 with C1, K20 with both strands, bring the working yarn to the front, PU (but do not knit) 2 two-strand sts from the cast on edge. Turn.

Row 25: Rearrange the sts so that the two C1 strands are in positions 1 and 2 on the left needle and the two MC strands are in positions 3 and 4. Pull on the tail ends until the sts are snug on the needle. K2 with C1, K2 with MC. Sl the 4 single strand sts back to the left needle.

Rows 26 - 27: K2 with C1, K2 with MC. Sl the 4 single strand sts back to the left needle.

Body

Section 1

The Cast On section counts as the first two rows the scarf. Start following the written instructions and the chart for the Section 1 at Row 3. In Section 1, MC is the Light color and C1 is the Dark color.

Dancing Circles Scarf Section

Row 3 (RS): K2 Dark, K2 Light, K20 Both, Sl WYIF x 2 Dark, Sl WYIF x 2 Light. 28 sts.

Row 4 (WS): K2 Light, K2 Dark, K8 Both, (K Dark, P Light) x 2, K10 Both, Sl WYIF x 2 Light, Sl WYIF x 2 Dark.

Row 5: K2 Dark, K2 Light, K9 Both, (K Light, P Dark) x 4, K7 Both, Sl WYIF x 2 Dark, Sl WYIF x 2 Light.

Row 6: K2 Light, K2 Dark, K6 Both, (K Dark, P Light) x 6, K8 Both, Sl WYIF x 2 Light, Sl WYIF x 2 Dark.

Row 7: K2 Dark, K2 Light, K8 Both, (K Light, P Dark) x 6, K6 Both, Sl WYIF x 2 Dark, Sl WYIF x 2 Light.

Rows 8 - 9: Repeat Rows 6 - 7.

Row 10: Repeat Row 6.

Row 11: K2 Dark, K2 Light, K8 Both, SSK Both, (K Light, P Dark) x 4, SSK Both, K6 Both, Sl WYIF x 2 Dark, Sl WYIF x 2 Light.

Row 12: K2 Light, K2 Dark, K7 Both, SSK Both, (K Dark, P Light) x 2, SSK Both, K5 Both, (K Light, P Dark) x 2, K2 Both, Sl WYIF x 2 Light, Sl WYIF x 2 Dark.

Row 13: K2 Dark, K2 Light, K1 Both, (K Dark, P Light) x 4, K5 Both, SSK x 2 Both, K8 Both, Sl WYIF x 2 Dark, Sl WYIF x 2 Light.

Row 14: K2 Light, K2 Dark, K15 Both, (K Light, P Dark) x 4, K1 Both, Sl WYIF x 2 Light, Sl WYIF x 2 Dark.

Row 15: Repeat Row 13.

Row 16: K2 Light, K2 Dark, K15 Both, SSK Both, (K Light, P Dark) x 2, SSK Both, K1 Both, Sl WYIF x 2 Light, Sl WYIF x 2 Dark.

Row 17: K2 Dark, K2 Light, K2 Both, SSK x 2 Both, K16 Both, Sl WYIF x 2 Dark, Sl WYIF x 2 Light.

Row 18: K2 Light, K2 Dark, K2 Both, (K Light, P Dark) x 2, K16 Both, Sl WYIF x 2 Light, Sl WYIF x 2 Dark.

Row 19: K2 Dark, K2 Light, K15 Both, (K Dark, P Light) x 4, K1 Both, Sl WYIF x 2 Dark, Sl WYIF x 2 Light.

Row 20: K2 Light, K2 Dark, K1 Both, (K Light, P Dark) x 4, K9 Both, (K Dark, P Light) x 2, K4 Both, Sl WYIF x 2 Light, Sl WYIF x 2 Dark.

Row 21: K2 Dark, K2 Light, K3 Both, (K Light, P Dark) x 4, K8 Both, (K Dark, P Light) x 4, K1 Both, Sl WYIF x 2 Dark, Sl WYIF x 2 Light.

Row 22: K2 Light, K2 Dark, K1 Both, SSK Both, (K Light, P Dark) x 2, SSK Both, K7 Both, (K Dark, P Light) x 6, K2 Both, Sl WYIF x 2 Light, Sl WYIF x 2 Dark.

Row 23: K2 Dark, K2 Light, K2 Both, (K Light, P Dark) x 6, K8 Both, SSK x 2 Both, K2 Both, Sl WYIF x 2 Dark, Sl WYIF x 2 Light.

Row 24: K2 Light, K2 Dark, K12 Both, (K Dark, P Light) x 6, K2 Both, Sl WYIF x 2 Light, Sl WYIF x 2 Dark.

Row 25: K2 Dark, K2 Light, K2 Both, (K Light, P Dark) x 6, K12 Both, Sl WYIF x 2 Dark, Sl WYIF x 2 Light.

Row 26: Repeat Row 24.

Row 27: K2 Dark, K2 Light, K2 Both, SSK Both, (K Light, P Dark) x 4, SSK Both, K12 Both, Sl WYIF x 2 Dark, Sl WYIF x 2 Light.

Row 28: K2 Light, K2 Dark, K6 Both, (K Light, P Dark) x 2, K5 Both, SSK Both, (K Dark, P Light) x 2, SSK Both, K3 Both, Sl WYIF x 2 Light, Sl WYIF x 2 Dark.

Row 29: K2 Dark, K2 Light, K4 Both, SSK x 2 Both, K5 Both, (K Dark, P Light) x 4, K5 Both, Sl WYIF x 2 Dark, Sl WYIF x 2 Light.

Row 30: K2 Light, K2 Dark, K5 Both, (K Light, P Dark) x 4, K11 Both, Sl WYIF x 2 Light, Sl WYIF x 2 Dark.

Row 31: K2 Dark, K2 Light, K11 Both, (K Dark, P Light) x 4, K5 Both, Sl WYIF x 2 Dark, Sl WYIF x 2 Light.

Row 32: K2 Light, K2 Dark, K5 Both, SSK Both, (K Light, P Dark) x 2, SSK Both, K11 Both, Sl WYIF x 2 Light, Sl WYIF x 2 Dark.

Row 33: K2 Dark, K2 Light, K12 Both, SSK x 2 Both, K6 Both, Sl WYIF x 2 Dark, Sl WYIF x 2 Light.1

Row 34: K2 Light, K2 Dark, K15 Both, (K Light, P Dark) x 2, K3 Both, Sl WYIF x 2 Light, Sl WYIF x 2 Dark.

Row 35: K2 Dark, K2 Light, K2 Both, (K Dark, P Light) x 4, K14 Both, Sl WYIF x 2 Dark, Sl WYIF x 2 Light.

Row 36: K2 Light, K2 Dark, K4 Both, (K Dark, P Light) x 2, K8 Both, (K Light, P Dark) x 4, K2 Both, Sl WYIF x 2 Light, Sl WYIF x 2 Dark.

Row 37: K2 Dark, K2 Light, K2 Both, (K Dark, P Light) x 4, K7 Both, (K Light, P Dark) x 4, K3 Both, Sl WYIF x 2 Dark, Sl WYIF x 2 Light.

Row 38: K2 Light, K2 Dark, K2 Both, (K Dark, P Light) x 6, K6 Both, SSK Both, (K Light, P Dark) x 2, SSK Both, K2 Both, Sl WYIF x 2 Light, Sl WYIF x 2 Dark.

Row 39: K2 Dark, K2 Light, K3 Both, SSK x 2 Both, K7 Both, (K Light, P Dark) x 6, K2 Both, Sl WYIF x 2 Dark, Sl WYIF x 2 Light.

Row 40: K2 Light, K2 Dark, K2 Both, (K Dark, P Light) x 6, K12 Both, Sl WYIF x 2 Light, Sl WYIF x 2 Dark.

Row 41: K2 Dark, K2 Light, K12 Both, (K Light, P Dark) x 6, K2 Both, Sl WYIF x 2 Dark, Sl WYIF x 2 Light.

Row 42: Repeat Row 40.

Row 43: K2 Dark, K2 Light, K12 Both, SSK Both, (K Light, P Dark) x 4, SSK Both, K2 Both, Sl WYIF x 2 Dark, Sl WYIF x 2 Light.

Row 44: K2 Light, K2 Dark, K3 Both, SSK Both, (K Dark, P Light) x 2, SSK Both, K6 Both, (K Dark, P Light) x 2, K5 Both, Sl WYIF x 2 Light, Sl WYIF x 2 Dark.

Row 45: K2 Dark, K2 Light, K4 Both, (K Light, P Dark) x 4, K6 Both, SSK x 2 Both, K4 Both, Sl WYIF x 2 Dark, Sl WYIF x 2 Light.

Row 46: K2 Light, K2 Dark, K11 Both, (K Dark, P Light) x 6, K3 Both, Sl WYIF x 2 Light, Sl WYIF x 2 Dark.

Row 47: K2 Dark, K2 Light, K3 Both, (K Light, P Dark) x 6, K11 Both, Sl WYIF x 2 Dark, Sl WYIF x 2 Light.

Rows 48 - 49: Repeat Rows 46 - 47.

Row 50: K2 Light, K2 Dark, K4 Both, (K Light, P Dark) x 2, K5 Both, (K Dark, P Light) x 6, K3 Both, Sl WYIF x 2 Light, Sl WYIF x 2 Dark.

Row 51: K2 Dark, K2 Light, K3 Both, SSK Both, (K Light, P Dark) x 4, SSK Both, K4 Both, (K Dark, P Light) x 4, K3 Both, Sl WYIF x 2 Dark, Sl WYIF x 2 Light.

Row 52: K2 Light, K2 Dark, K3 Both, (K Light, P Dark) x 4, K5 Both, SSK Both, (K Dark, P Light) x 2, SSK Both, K4 Both, Sl WYIF x 2 Light, Sl WYIF x 2 Dark.

Row 53: K2 Dark, K2 Light, K5 Both, SSK x 2 Both, K6 Both, (K Dark, P Light) x 4, K3 Both, Sl WYIF x 2 Dark, Sl WYIF x 2 Light.

Row 54: K2 Light, K2 Dark, K3 Both, SSK Both, (K Light, P Dark) x 2, SSK Both, K13 Both, Sl WYIF x 2 Light, Sl WYIF x 2 Dark.

Row 55: K2 Dark, K2 Light, K14 Both, SSK x 2 Both, K4 Both, Sl WYIF x 2 Dark, Sl WYIF x 2 Light.

Row 56: K2 Light, K2 Dark, K20 Both, Sl WYIF x 2 Light, Sl WYIF x 2 Dark.

Section 2
Cut the MC, leaving a tail to weave in. Color C1 becomes the Light.
Add C2 as the new Dark color.

Row 1 (RS): K2 Dark, K2 Light, K20 Both, Sl WYIF x 2 Dark, Sl WYIF x 2 Light. 28 sts.

Row 2 (WS): K2 Light, K2 Dark, K20 Both, Sl WYIF x 2 Light, Sl WYIF x 2 Dark.

Work Rows 3 to 56 of the pattern.

Section 3
Cut the C1, leaving a tail to weave in. Color C2 becomes the Light.
Add C3 as the new Dark color.
Work Rows 1 to 56 of the pattern.

Section 4
Cut the C2, leaving a tail to weave in. Color C3 becomes the Light.
Add C4 as the new Dark color.
Work Rows 1 to 56 of the pattern.

Section 5
Cut the C4, leaving a tail to weave in. Color C2 becomes the Light. Add C3 as the new Dark color.
Work Rows 1 to 56 of the pattern.

Section 6
Cut the C3, leaving a tail to weave in. Color C1 becomes the Light.
Add C2 as the new Dark color.
Work Rows 1 to 56 of the pattern.

Section 7
Cut the C2, leaving a tail to weave in. Color MC becomes the Light. Add C1 as the new Dark color.
Work Rows 1 to 56 of the pattern.

Bind Off
Rows 1 - 3: K2 with C1, K2 with MC, Sl the 4 single strand sts back to the left needle.

Row 4: K2 with C1, K1 with MC, SSK the last I-cord st with the first two-strand st of the previous row, Sl the 4 single strand sts back to the left needle.

Rows 5 - 23: K2 with C1, K1 with MC, SSK the last I-cord st with the next two-strand st of the previous row, Sl the 4 single strand sts back to the left needle.

Rows 24 - 25: K2 with C1, K2 with MC, Sl the 4 single strand sts back to the left needle.

Sl these 4 sts onto the right needle as if you were knitting 4 together. Kitchener stitch together the two pairs of C1 sts and the two pairs of 2 MC sts.

Finishing
Weave ends into the I-cord edges, wash and lay flat to dry.

Dancing Circles Scarf

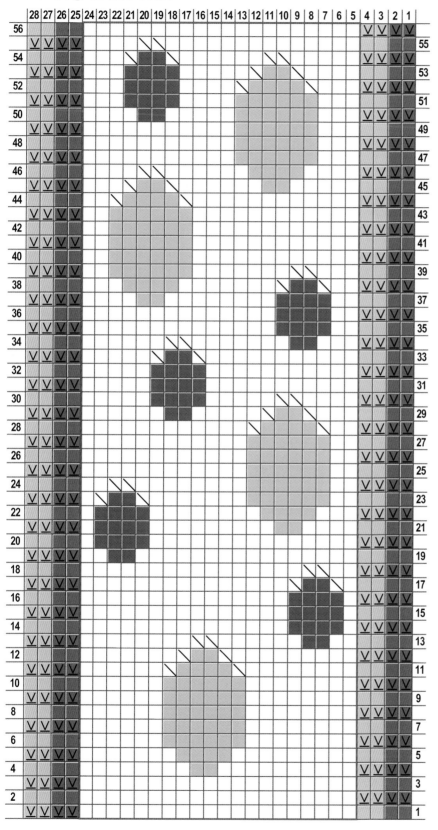

Legend:

☐	knit with both yarn colors
⩗	**slip wyif** Slip stitch as if to purl, with yarn in front
◹	**ssk** Slip each of the strands in the double knit pair individually as if to knit. Insert left-hand needle into front of these 2 stitches and knit them together
■	Dark - I-Cord
▨	Light - I-Cord
■	RS: k Dark, p Light WS: k Light, p Dark
▨	RS: k Light, p Dark WS: k Dark, p Light
☐	Body of the scarf

Section 7
MC = Light
C1 = Dark

Section 6
C1 = Light
C2 = Dark

Section 5
C2 = Light
C3 = Dark

Section 4
C3 = Light
C4 = Dark

Section 3
C2 = Light
C3 = Dark

Section 2
C1 = Light
C2 = Dark

Section 1
MC = Light
C1 = Dark

APHRA COWL

by Claire Slade

FINISHED MEASUREMENTS
8.75" high x 22.5" (44.75") circumference

YARN
Knit Picks Chroma Twist Fingering (70% Superwash Wool, 30% Nylon; 437 yards/100g): MC Natural 27253; C1 Surfs Up 27256 1 skein each.

NEEDLES
US 2.5 (3mm) 16" (32") circular needle or size to obtain gauge.

US 2 (2.75mm) 16" (32)" circular needle, or 1 size smaller than needle to obtain gauge.

NOTIONS
Yarn Needle
1 Stitch Marker

GAUGE
30 sts and 60 rows = 4" over Slipped Stitch Pattern in the round on larger needles, lightly blocked

Aphra Cowl

Notes:

This cowl is knit entirely in the round from the bottom up. Only one yarn is used at a time with the pattern being created with slipped stitches. It is important when slipping stitches to slip them one at a time and not pull the yarn too tightly across the back of the work as this will cause puckering.

When working the chart, read each row from right to left, as a RS row.

Slipped Stitch Pattern (in the round over multiples of 4 sts)

Rnds 1-2: Using C1 *K1, Sl1 P-wise WYIB; rep from * to end.

Rnds 3-4: Using MC *Sl1 P-wise WYIB, K1; rep from * to end.

Rnds 5-6: Using C1 *K3, Sl1 P-wise WYIB; rep from * to end.

Rnds 7-8: Using MC *Sl3 P-wise WYIB, K1; rep from * to end.

Rnds 9-10: Using C1 K.

Rnds 11-12: Using MC *Sl1 P-wise WYIB, K1, Sl2 P-wise WYIB; rep from * to end.

Rnds 13-14: Using C1 *K1, Sl1 P-wise WYIB, K2; rep from * to end.

Rnds 15-16: Using MC *Sl1 P-wise WYIB, K1; rep from * to end.

Rnds 17-18: Using C1 *K1, Sl1 P-wise WYIB; rep from * to end.

Rnds 19-20: Using MC K.

DIRECTIONS

Lower Edging

Using MC and smaller needles CO 168 (336) sts, join to work in the rnd being careful not to twist, PM to mark beginning of rnd.

Rnd 1: K.

Rnd 2: P.

Rnd 3-4: Rep Rnds 1-2.

Change to larger needles.

Rnds 5-6: K.

Main Section

Join C1 and work Rnds 1-20 of Slipped Stitch Pattern a total of 6 times, following either the line-by-line instructions or the chart.

Break C1.

Upper Edging

Change to smaller needles.

Rnd 1: P.

Rnd 2: K.

Rep Rnds 1-2 once more.

BO all sts.

Finishing

Weave in ends, wash and block lightly to stated measurements.

Legend:

☐	**knit**	knit stitch
V	**slip**	Slip stitch as if to purl, holding yarn in back
☐	MC	
■	C1	

Aphra Cowl Chart

4	3	2	1	
MC	MC	MC	MC	20
MC	MC	MC	MC	19
V (MC)	C1	V (MC)	C1	18
V (MC)	C1	V (MC)	C1	17
MC	V (C1)	C1	V (C1)	16
MC	V (C1)	C1	V (C1)	15
C1	C1	V (MC)	MC	14
C1	C1	V (MC)	MC	13
V (C1)	V (C1)	MC	V (C1)	12
V (C1)	V (C1)	MC	V (C1)	11
C1	C1	C1	MC	10
C1	C1	C1	MC	9
MC	V (C1)	V (C1)	V (C1)	8
MC	V (C1)	V (C1)	V (C1)	7
V (C1)	C1	MC	MC	6
V (C1)	C1	MC	MC	5
MC	V (C1)	MC	V (C1)	4
MC	V (C1)	MC	V (C1)	3
V (C1)	C1	V (MC)	MC	2
V (C1)	C1	V (MC)	MC	1

ENTWINED OMBRÉ SLOUCH

by Emily Kintigh

FINISHED MEASUREMENTS
20 (22, 24)" brim circumference x 9.25 (11.5, 11.75)" tall

YARN
Knit Picks Stroll Gradient (75% Superwash Merino Wool, 25% Nylon; 458 yards/100g): Deep Dive 27369, 1 skein

NEEDLES
US 1 (2.25mm) 16" circular needles, or two sizes smaller than needle to obtain gauge
US 3 (3.25mm) 16" circular needles and DPNs or two 24" circular needles for two circulars technique, or one 32" or longer circular needle for Magic Loop technique, or size to obtain gauge

NOTIONS
Yarn Needle
Removable Stitch Markers
Cable Needle

GAUGE
36 sts and 35 rows = 4" over Entwined Chart in the round on larger needles, blocked
32 sts = 4" in 2x2 Ribbing on smaller needles, blocked

Entwined Ombré Slouch

Notes:

Before knitting the hat, wind yarn into two equal balls starting from the outside of the cake. The first ball is the C1 and is worked from light blue to lime green and the second ball is the MC and is worked from dark blue to light blue. To wind center pull cakes instead, start from the center of the cake and wind the yarn into two equal center pull cakes. The first is the MC and is worked from dark blue to light blue. The second is the C1 and is worked from light blue to lime green.

The twists are worked in two colors. The knitted stitch is worked in the MC and the purled stitch is worked in the C1 as indicated in the chart legend.

The main hat circumference is a bit larger than the brim circumference. The hat circumference above the brim is approximately 21.25 (24, 26.5)".

When working the charts, each chart row is read from right to left, as a RS row.

2x2 Ribbing (in the round over a multiple of 4 sts)
Rnd 1: (K2, P2) to end.
Repeat Rnd 1 for pattern.

DIRECTIONS
Brim

With smaller needles and MC, loosely CO 160 (176, 192) sts. PM and join in the rnd being careful not to twist the sts.
Work in 2x2 Ribbing until piece measures 1.5 (1.75, 2)" from CO edge.

Main Hat

Switch to larger needles.

Size 20":
Rnd 1: (K5, M1) to end. 192 sts.

Size 22":
Rnd 1: *(K4, M1) four times, K6, M1; rep from * to end. 216 sts.

Size 24":
Rnd 1: (K4, M1) to end. 240 sts.

All Sizes:
Set up Rnd: *With C1, K1, with MC, K2, with C1, K3; rep from * to end.

Begin working from Entwined Chart repeating the chart over all sts except on Rnds 3, 4 and 11 where the last few sts differ from the repeat as indicated on the chart. The beginning of the Rnd moves on Rnd 3, then again on Rnd 11.

At the end of Rnd 3: Work to the last st, place next st on CN, hold in back, remove marker, with MC, K1, with C1, P1 from CN, place marker. This is now the beginning of the rnd.

At the end of Rnd 11: Work to the last st, move the marker here, making this the new beginning of the rnd. The next stitch is now the first st of Rnd 12.

Repeat the chart 3 times before moving on to Crown Shaping.

Crown Shaping

Switch to DPNs, or two 24" circular needles for two circulars technique, or one 32" or longer circular needle for Magic Loop technique when the stitches no longer fit comfortably on the 16" circular needle.

Note: When working the Crown Decreases Chart, the beginning of the rnd moves on Rnd 3, and the end of Rnd 4 is different than the rest of the rnd. Otherwise, repeat the chart across the entire rnd. At the end of Rnd 3, work to last st, place next st on CN, hold in back, remove marker, with MC, K1, with C1, P1 from CN, place marker. This is now the beginning of the rnd.

Size 20":
Work Crown Decreases Chart.
Cut yarn and pull through remaining sts.

Size 22":
Work Rnds 1-12 of Entwined Chart once more.
Work Larger Sizes Decrease Chart, working the 6 st repeat 7 times before continuing to work the rest of the chart. The chart is repeated four times across the rnd. 192 sts.
Work Crown Decreases Chart.
Cut yarn and pull through remaining sts.

Size 24":
Work Rnds 1-12 of Entwined Chart once more.
Work Larger Sizes Decrease Chart, working the 6 st repeat 3 times before continuing to work the rest of the chart. The chart is repeated eight times across the rnd. 192 sts.
Work Crown Decreases Chart.
Cut yarn and pull through remaining sts.

Finishing

Weave in ends, wash and block.

Crown Decreases Chart

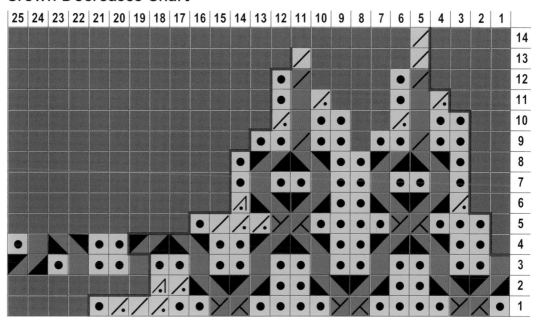

Legend:

	knit
☐	knit stitch
⊡	**purl**
	purl stitch

Right Twist
Skip the first stitch, knit into 2nd stitch, then knit skipped stitch. Slip both stitches from needle together.

p2tog
Purl 2 stitches together

k2tog
Knit two stitches together as one stitch

p3tog
Purl three stitches together as one

☐ **repeat**

▦ MC

▦ C1

Right Twist, purl bg
sl1 to CN, hold in back. With MC k1. With C1, p1 from CN

Left Twist, purl bg
sl1 to CN, hold in front. With C1, p1. With MC, k1 from CN

Entwined Chart

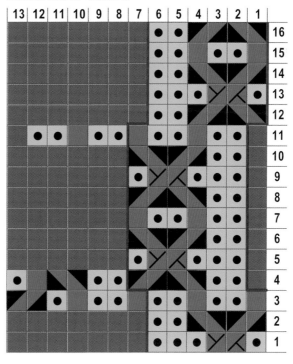

Larger Sizes Decreases Chart

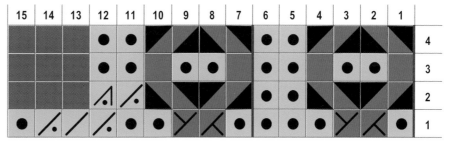

GRADEN PULLOVER

by Helen Metcalfe

FINISHED MEASUREMENTS

32.75 (38, 40.5, 45.5, 48, 53, 58, 60.75, 65.75)" finished bust measurement; garment is meant to be worn with 3-4" of positive ease

YARN

Knit Picks Swish Worsted (100% Superwash Merino Wool; 110 yards/50g): MC White 24662, 8 (9, 10, 11, 12, 13, 14, 15, 16) balls; C1 Serrano 24663, 1 ball; C2 Hollyberry 25148, C3 Amethyst Heather 25147, C4 Sugar Plum 25142, 1 (1, 1, 2, 2, 2, 2, 2, 2) balls each

NEEDLES

US 7 (4.5mm) 24" circular needle, plus DPNs or two 24" circular needles for two circulars technique or size to obtain gauge

US 8 (5mm) 24" circular needle, plus DPNs or two 24" circular needles for two circulars technique, or size to obtain gauge

NOTIONS

4 Stitch Markers
Scrap Yarn
Yarn Needle

GAUGE

19 sts and 21 rows = 4" over Fair Isle Pattern worked in the round on larger needles, blocked
23 sts = 4" in K1, P1 Rib on smaller needles in the round, blocked

Graden Pullover

Notes:

This sweater is knitted seamlessly from the bottom up with a Fair Isle pattern around the bottom and sleeve hems. Short rows are used to shape front neckline while underarm sts are bound off using the 3-Needle BO technique. The chart rows are read from right to left as RS rows, and repeated across the round.

K1, P1 Rib (worked in the rnd over multiples of 2 sts)
All Rnds: *K1, P1; rep from * to end.

Wrap and Turn (W&T): Tutorial on Knit Picks website can be found at http://tutorials.knitpicks.com/wptutorials/short-rows-wrap-and-turn-or-wt/

3-Needle Bind Off
*Hold the two pieces of knitting together with the points facing to the right. Insert a third needle into the first st on each of the needles K-wise, starting with the front needle. Work a K st, pulling the loop through both of the sts you've inserted the third needle through. After pulling the loop through, slip the first st off of each of the needles. Repeat from *. Pass the first finished st over the second and off of the needle.

DIRECTIONS

Body

The body is worked in the round from the hem up. It is then placed on hold while the sleeves are completed, before joining all three pieces for the yoke.

Hem

Using smaller circular needle and MC, loosely CO 156 (180, 192, 216, 228, 252, 276, 288, 312) sts. Join to work in the rnd, being careful not to twist. PM to mark beginning of rnd.
Work in K1, P1 Rib for 2" from CO edge.

Main Body

Change to larger circular needle and K 1 rnd in MC. Break MC.
Work Rnds 1- 39 of chart.
Cont in St st (K all rnds) using MC until work measures 18.25 (18.25, 18.25, 18, 17.5, 17.25, 16.75, 16.75, 16.5)" from CO edge.
Next Rnd: Remove M, place 4 (5, 6, 7, 8, 9, 10, 11, 12) sts on scrap yarn, K70 (80, 84, 94, 98, 108, 118, 122, 132) sts for Front, place 8 (10, 12, 14, 16, 18, 20, 22, 24) sts on scrap yarn, K to last 4 (5, 6, 7, 8, 9, 10, 11, 12) sts, place 4 (5, 6, 7, 8, 9, 10, 11, 12) sts on scrap yarn. 140 (160, 168, 188, 196, 216, 236, 244, 264) sts
Set aside and work sleeves.

Sleeves (make 2 the same)

The sleeves are worked in the round from the wrists up.

Hem

Using smaller DPNs and MC, loosely CO 40 (42, 46, 48, 52, 52, 54, 54, 56) sts. Join to work in the rnd, being careful not to twist. PM to mark beginning of rnd.
Work in K1, P1 Rib for 1.5" from CO edge.

Body of Sleeve

Change to larger DPNs and using MC, K 1 rnd. Break MC.
Next Rnd: Work chart Rnd 1 starting with chart st 11 (10, 8, 1, 11, 11, 10, 10, 9).

Inc Rnd: K1, M1, work chart to last st, M1, K1. 2 sts inc.
Cont to work to end of chart, then cont in St st in MC. At the same time rep Inc Rnd every 11 (11, 11, 10, 8, 6, 5, 4, 4) rnds a total of 8 (8, 8, 9, 11, 16, 18, 22, 23) times, until there are 56 (58, 62, 66, 74, 84, 90, 98, 102) sts.
Cont without shaping until work measures 19.5 (20, 20, 20.5, 20.5, 21, 21, 21.5, 21.5)" from CO edge.
Next Rnd: Remove M, place 4 (5, 6, 7, 8, 9, 10, 11, 12) sts on scrap yarn, K to last 4 (5, 6, 7, 8, 9, 10, 11, 12) sts, place 4 (5, 6, 7, 8, 9, 10, 11, 12) sts on scrap yarn. 48 (48, 50, 52, 58, 66, 70, 76, 78) sts.
Set aside and work second sleeve.

Yoke

Join body and sleeves.
Next Rnd: Using larger circular needle and MC, K sts from first sleeve, PM, K sts from front, PM, K sts from second sleeve, PM and K sts from back. PM to mark end of rnd. 236 (256, 268, 292, 312, 348, 376, 396, 420) sts.

Dec Rnd: SM, K1, SSK, *K to 3 sts before M, K2tog, K1, SM, K1, SSK, rep from * twice more, K to last 3 sts, K2tog, K1. 8 sts dec.
R.Rep Dec Rnd followed by three plain K rnds a total of 3 (3, 4, 4, 4, 5, 5, 6, 6) times. 212 (232, 236, 260, 280, 308, 336, 348, 372) sts.

Rep Dec Rnd followed by one plain K rnd a total of 7 (8, 8, 9, 10, 10, 11, 10, 12) times. 156 (168, 172, 188, 200, 228, 248, 268, 276) sts. 28 (26, 26, 26, 30, 36, 38, 44, 42) sts in each sleeve section, 50 (58, 60, 68, 70, 78, 86, 90, 96) sts each in front and back.
Remove markers.

Neckline Shaping

Short Row 1 (RS): K41 (43, 43, 47, 51, 61, 66, 74, 74) sts, W&T, now working flat.
Short Row 2 (WS): P until 23 (23, 25, 25, 27, 27, 29, 29, 31) sts remain before W&T, W&T. 132 (144, 146, 162, 172, 200, 218, 238, 244) sts.
Short Row 3 (RS): K11 (12, 12, 13, 13, 14, 14, 15, 16), PM, *K2tog, K2; rep from * 8 (9, 9, 10, 11, 14, 16, 18, 18) times in total, K2tog - (-, -, 1, 1, 1, 1, 1, 1) more time, PM, K46 (48, 50, 52, 54, 56, 58, 60, 64), PM *K2tog, K2; rep from * 8 (9, 9, 10, 11, 14, 16, 18, 18) times in total, K2tog - (-, -, 1, 1, 1, 1, 1, 1) more time, K7 (8, 8, 8, 9, 9, 10, 10), W&T. 112 (122, 124, 135, 143, 165, 179, 195, 200) sts.
Short Row 4: P to 4 (4, 4, 5, 5, 5, 5, 6) sts before W&T, W&T. 108 (118, 120, 130, 138, 160, 174, 190, 194) sts.
Short Row 5 (RS): K to M, SM, *K2tog, K1; rep from * to - (-, -, 1, 1, 1, 1, 1, 1) st before M, K- (-, -, 1, 1, 1, 1, 1, 1), SM, K to M, SM, *K2tog, K1; rep from * to - (-, -, 1, 1, 1, 1, 1, 1) st before M, K- (-, -, 1, 1, 1, 1, 1, 1), SM, K4 (4, 4, 4, 5, 5, 5, 5), W&T. 88 (96, 98, 106, 112, 127, 137, 149, 153) sts.
Short Row 6: P to 4 (4, 4, 4, 5, 5, 5, 5) sts before W&T, W&T. 84 (92, 94, 102, 108, 122, 132, 144, 148) sts.
Short Row 7 (RS): K to M, remove M, *K2tog; rep from * to - (-, -, 1, 1, 1, 1, 1, 1) st before M, K- (-, -, 1, 1, 1, 1, 1, 1), SM, K to M, SM, *K2tog; rep from * to - (-, -, 1, 1, 1, 1, 1, 1) st before M, K- (-, -, 1, 1, 1, 1, 1, 1), remove M, W&T. 65 (70, 72, 78, 82, 90, 96, 103, 107) sts.
Short Row 8: P to 3 (4, 4, 4, 4, 4, 5, 5) sts before W&T, W&T. 62 (66, 68, 74, 78, 86, 92, 98, 102) sts.

Short Row 9 (RS): K2 (1, 1, 1, 2, 1, 1, 1), *K2tog; rep from * to M, remove M, K to M, remove M, *K2tog; rep from * to 2 (1, 1, 1, 2, 1, 1, 1, 1) st(s) before end, K1 (-, -, -, 1, -, -, -, -), W&T. 55 (57, 59, 63, 67, 71, 75, 79, 83) sts.

Short Row 10: P to last st, W&T. (54, 56, 58, 62, 66, 70, 74, 78, 82) sts.

Neckband

Return to working in the rnd.

Next Rnd: K all 102 (106, 110, 116, 122, 128, 134, 140, 148) sts, closing wraps across rnd. PM to mark end of rnd.

Next Rnd: *K2tog 5 (5, 5, 6, 7, 8, 9, 10, 10) times, K41 (43, 45, 46, 47, 48, 49, 50, 54); rep from * once more. 92 (96, 100, 104, 108, 112, 116, 120, 128) sts.

Change to smaller DPNs.

Work in K1, P1 Rib for 7 rnds.

Loosely BO.

Finishing

Join underarm sts by returning held sts to needles (sleeve sts on one needle and body sts on another) and working a 3-Needle BO. Repeat for second underarm. Weave in ends, wash and block to diagram.

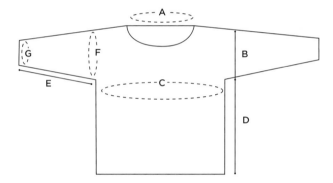

A 16 (16.75, 17.25, 18, 18.75, 19.5, 20.25, 20.75, 22.25)"
B 7 (7.5, 8.25, 8.75, 9, 9.75, 10.25, 10.5, 11.25)"
C 32.75 (38, 40.5, 45.5, 48, 53, 58, 60.75, 65.75)"
D 18.25 (18.25, 18.25, 18, 17.5, 17.25, 16.75, 16.75, 16.5)"
E 19.5 (20, 20, 20.5, 20.5, 21, 21, 21.5, 21.5)"
F 11.75 (12.25, 13, 14, 15.5, 17.75, 19, 20.75, 21.5)"
G 7 (7.25, 8, 8.25, 9, 9, 9.5, 9.75)

Graden Chart

12	11	10	9	8	7	6	5	4	3	2	1	
												39
												38
												37
												36
												35
												34
												33
												32
												31
												30
												29
												28
												27
												26
												25
												24
												23
												22
												21
												20
												19
												18
												17
												16
												15
												14
												13
												12
												11
												10
												9
												8
												7
												6
												5
												4
												3
												2
												1

Legend:

knit
knit stitch

☐ MC

■ C1

■ C2

■ C3

■ C4

OMBRÉ KNIT QUILT

by Melina Martin Gingras

FINISHED MEASUREMENTS
64x84"

YARN
Knit Picks Brava Worsted (100% Premium Acrylic; 218 yards/100g): C1 White 25694, 4 balls; C2 Mint 26120, 6 balls; C3 Cornflower 25708, 4 balls; C4 Tranquil 25710, 4 balls; C5 Marina 26131, 5 balls; C6 Peacock 26127, 6 balls

NEEDLES
US 7 (4.5mm) straight or circular needles plus 40" or longer circular needle for Border, or size to obtain gauge

NOTIONS
Yarn Needle

GAUGE
18 sts and 36 rows = 4" in Garter stitch, lightly steam blocked

Ombré Knit Quilt

Notes:

My mother is an avid quilter, but as someone who only dabbles in sewing, I just don't have the patience for quilting. Because I love a lot of her traditional quilt designs, I have always been interested in how I could turn a quilt into a knit or crochet blanket design. The Ombre Knit Quilt does just that.

Inspired by a modular quilt, the Ombre Knit Quilt is knit in a modular fashion starting with 10x10" squares that consists of five 2" Garter stitch stripes. Once the first square is complete, the knitter picks up and knits stitches on the side of the square in order to construct the subsequent squares in each section. Each section consists of two squares that have five strips of alternating colors, which are seamed together in long rows, and then the rows are seamed together. A modular border is added once all the strips are joined together, by picking up and knitting 2" of Garter stitch on the long sides first, then doing the same at the top and bottom of the blanket.

For ease of joining sections and picking up sts, slip the first st of every row except on the first row of a color change. It is easiest to weave in ends as you go along or when you finish each section. Make sure all your color changes happen on the same side, and that all your edges line up.

Garter Stitch (worked flat)
All Rows: Knit.
2 rows of Garter Stitch equals 1 Garter stitch ridge.

Color Stripe Pattern
Work 9 ridges of Garter Stitch (18 rows) in specified color.

DIRECTIONS
Section 1 (Make 4)
First Square: CO 45 sts in C1. *Work Color Stripe Pattern in C1, work Color Stripe Pattern in C2; rep from * once more, work Color Stripe Pattern in C1. BO all sts loosely.
Second Square: With RS facing, using C1, PU and K 45 sts alongside of finished square, so that new stripes will be worked perpendicularly to stripes from First Square of Section 1. *Work Color Stripe Pattern in C1, work Color Stripe Pattern in C2; rep from * once more, work Color Stripe Pattern in C3. BO all sts loosely.

Section 1 Diagram

Section 2 (Make 4)
First Square: Rep Section 1 First Square.

Second Square: With RS facing, using C2, PU and K 45 sts alongside of finished square, so that new stripes will be worked perpendicularly to stripes from First Square of Section 2. *Work Color Stripe Pattern in C2, work Color Stripe Pattern in C1; rep from * once more, work Color Stripe Pattern in C2. BO all sts loosely.

Section 2 Diagram

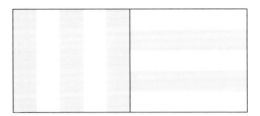

Section 3 (Make 4)
First Square: CO 45 sts in C3. *Work Color Stripe Pattern in C3, work Color Stripe Pattern in C2; rep from * once more, work Color Stripe Pattern in C3. BO all sts loosely.
Second Square: With RS facing, using C3, PU and K 45 sts alongside of finished square, so that new stripes will be worked perpendicularly to stripes from First Square of Section 3. *Work Color Stripe Pattern in C3, work Color Stripe Pattern in C4; rep from * once more, work Color Stripe Pattern in C5. BO all sts loosely.

Section 3 Diagram

Section 4 (Make 4)
First Square: CO 45 sts in C4. *Work Color Stripe Pattern in C4, work Color Stripe Pattern in C3; rep from * once more, work Color Stripe Pattern in C4. BO all sts loosely.
Second Square: With RS facing, using C4, PU and K 45 sts alongside of finished square, so that stripes will be worked perpendicularly to stripes from First Square of Section 4. Work Color Stripe Pattern in C4, *work Color Stripe Pattern in C3, work Color Strip Pattern in C2; rep from * once more. BO all sts loosely.

Section 4 Diagram

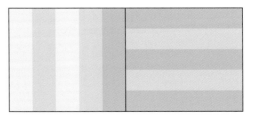

Section 5 (Make 4)

First Square: CO 45 sts in C5. *Work Color Stripe Pattern in C5, work Color Stripe Pattern in C4; rep from * once more, work Color Stripe Pattern in C5. BO all sts loosely.

Second Square: With RS facing, using C5, PU and K 45 sts alongside of finished square, so that stripes will be worked perpendicularly to stripes from First Square of Section 5. *Work Color Stripe Pattern in C5, work Color Stripe Pattern in C6; rep from * once more, work Color Stripe Pattern in C5. BO all sts loosely.

Section 5 Diagram

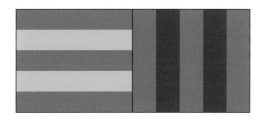

Section 6 (Make 4)

First Square: CO 45 sts in C6. *Work Color Stripe Pattern in C6, work Color Stripe Pattern in C5; rep from * once more, work Color Stripe Pattern in C6. BO all sts loosely.

Second Square: With RS facing, using C6, PU and K 45 sts alongside of finished square, so that stripes will be worked perpendicularly to stripes from First Square of Section 6. Work Color Stripe Pattern in C6, *work Color Stripe Pattern in C5, work Color Stripe Pattern in C4; rep from * once more. BO all sts loosely.

Section 6 Diagram

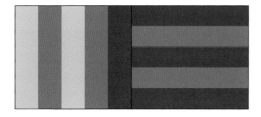

Finishing

Seaming

Making sure all color changes stay on the same side, seam one of each Section into sets of two rows as follows:

Row 1: Section 1, Section 3, Section 5.
See Row Diagram
Row 2: Section 2, Section 4, Section 6.
See Row 2 Diagram
*Once all sections have been seamed, seam Row 1 to the top of Row 2; rep from * three more times.
See Seamed Diagram
Seam the resulting 4 identical strips together, Row 1 on top.
Weave in all ends.

Border

Using C6 with RS facing and long circular needle, PU and K sts along a long edge of the quilt. PU one st for every ridge, and one st for each seam.

Work 9 ridges in Garter stitch and BO loosely. Rep on the opposite side.

With RS facing, PU and K sts along the top of the quilt. PU one st for every st, and one st for every seam.

Work 9 ridges in Garter stitch and BO loosely. Rep on the bottom.

Weave in ends. Lightly steam to block.

Row 1 Diagram

Row 2 Diagram

Seamed Diagram

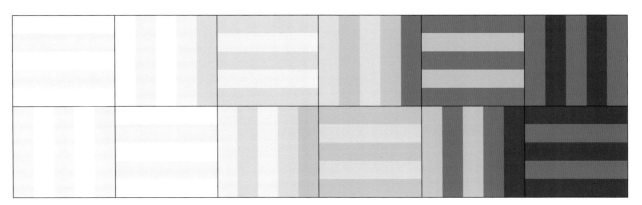

DISSIPATE COWL

by Amanda Bjoerge

FINISHED MEASUREMENTS

6-Color Long Cowl: 48.5" circumference x 6" high; 3-Color Short Cowl: 22.5" circumference x 8.75" high

YARN

Knit Picks Alpaca Cloud Lace (100% Baby Alpaca; 440 yards/50g): A Sophia 26795, B Iris Heather 23506, C Foxtrot Heather 24418, D Diana 26762, E Edgar 26787, F Thomas 26800, 1 skein each

NEEDLES

US 4 (3.5mm) 16" circular needle, or long circular for Magic Loop method, or size to obtain gauge

NOTIONS

Yarn Needle
Stitch Markers

GAUGE

20 sts and 28 rows = 4" in Trinity St Pattern with yarn held double, blocked. (Gauge for this project is approximate)

For pattern support, contact bjoergeknits@gmail.com

Dissipate Cowl

Notes:

Simple but elegant cowl, knit using 2 strands of lace weight yarn to create a gradual shift or dissipation of color. This cowl uses the trinity stitch to create an elegant lacework while still being at the beginner/intermediate lace level. Beginner knitters might want to use lifelines, which is a piece of waste yarn threaded through a row to hold the stitches. This way if you need to undo your work to correct a mistake, you can always go back to your last lifeline and pick up the stitches and continue from that point. Both 3-color and 6-color cowls are easily increased in length and width by adding additional repeats.

Note that this cowl (both sizes) is knit using 2 strands of lace weight yarn. I will denote how many strands of which color by the following method: 1 strand of color A, 1 strand of color B = A1B1; 2 strands of color A = A2.

Here are a couple of tips to help keep all of your strands from tangling. If you are working each color from 1 ball of yarn, I suggest putting the ball in a small plastic bag with a hole in the bottom. Pull the center pull strand out of this hole, and let the other strand, that will circle around the ball come out of the top. You can also use a twist tie or rubber band to keep the ball from falling out while still leaving enough room for yarn to easily be pulled. When using only one strand of a color, use the center pull strand.

1into3: (K1, YO, K1) into 1 st. 2 sts inc.

Trinity Stitch Pattern (worked flat over multiples of 8 sts plus 2)
Row 1: Sl 1, (Sk2p, 1into3) to M, lock color, (Sk2p, 1into3) to last st, K1.
Row 2: Sl 1, P all sts.
Row 3: Sl 1, (1into3, Sk2p) to M, lock color, (1into3, Sk2p,) to last st, K1.
Row 4: Sl 1, P all sts.
Rep Rows 1-4 for pattern.

Trinity Stitch Pattern (in the rnd over multiples of 4 sts)
Rnd 1: (Sk2p, 1into3) to end.
Rnd 2: K all sts.
Rnd 3: (1into3, Sk2p) to end.
Rnd 4: K all sts.
Rep Rnds 1-4 for pattern.

Lock Color (Row 1/Rnd 1): Sl 1, insert needle into the next 2 sts as if to knit, bring strands you wish to lock over the RH needle, right to left. K2tog with working yarn so that the st is pulled under carried strand. Pass slipped st over with the carried strand down, so that it becomes locked in.
Lock Color (Row 3/Rnd 3): Insert needle into st as if to knit, bring strands you wish to lock over the RH needle, right to left. Knit into st with working yarn so that the st is pulled under carried strand. YO, K1 into the same st with working yarn, with the carried strand down, so that it becomes locked in.
Lock Color K-wise (Rows 2 & 4): Insert needle into st as if to knit, bring strands you wish to lock over the RH needle, right to left. Knit into st with working yarn so that the st is pulled under

carried strand. Work the next st normally, with carried strand down, so that it becomes locked in.
Lock Color P-wise (Rows 2 & 4): Insert needle into st as if to purl, bring stands you with to lock over the RH needle, right to left. Purl into st with working yarn so that the st is pulled under carried strand. Work the next st normally, with carried strand down, so that it becomes locked in.

Jeny's Surprisingly Stretchy Bind Off
Wrap working yarn around right needle the opposite way from a traditional yarn over, K1. YO plus one st on the RH needle. Just like in a traditional BO, insert left needle into YO (2nd st on RH needle) and pass it over the first st. *Reverse YO, K1, P2SSO; rep from * to end.

DIRECTIONS
Short 3-Color Cowl
The 3-color version of the cowl is worked in the round.
Using a long tail CO (or preferred CO), CO 112 sts with 2 strands of color A. PM to denote the beginning of the rnd and join for knitting in the rnd, taking care not to twist the work.

Color Shift
I like to weave in the ends of the color shift as I knit, but you are also welcome to weave them in at the end. You will shift colors every 12 rounds (3 reps of the Trinity St Pattern).

Chart instructions are as follows:
Work Rows 1-4 of Circular Trinity Stitch Chart 3 times.
Work Rows 5-8 of Circular Trinity Stitch Chart 3 times.
Work Rows 9-12 of Circular Trinity Stitch Chart 3 times.
Work Rows 13-16 of Circular Trinity Stitch Chart 3 times.
Work Rows 17-20 of Circular Trinity Stitch Chart 3 times.

Written instructions are as follows:
Rnds 1-12: Work the Trinity Stitch Pattern given above in A2, rep 3 times.
Rnds 13-24: Work the Trinity Stitch Pattern given above in A1B1, rep 3 times.
Rnds 25-36: Work the Trinity Stitch Pattern given above in B2, rep 3 times.
Rnds 37-48: Work the Trinity Stitch Pattern given above in B1C1, rep 3 times.
Rnds 49-60: Work the Trinity Stitch Pattern given above in C2, rep 3 times.

BO all sts using Jeny's Surprisingly Stretchy BO or preferred stretchy BO.

Finishing
Weave in ends, wash and block.

Long 6-Color Cowl
The 6-color version of the cowl is worked flat, then seamed together.
Using a long tail CO (or preferred CO), CO 121 sts with A2, PM, CO 121 sts with C1D1. 242 sts.
Sl 1, K to M with C1D1, SM, lock C1D1 K-wise, K to end with A2.
You will work a vertical color shift every 8 rows, 2 reps of the Trinity St Pattern.

Color Shift

I like to weave in the ends of the color shift as I knit, but you are also welcome to weave them in at the end. Both written and charted instructions are given below. If using the charted version, remember to lock the yarn at the color switch, instructions are given above.

To work from the chart:
Work Rows 1-4 of the Flat Trinity Dissipate chart twice.
Work Rows 5-8 of the Flat Trinity Dissipate chart twice.
Work Rows 9-12 of the Flat Trinity Dissipate chart twice.
Work Rows 13-16 of the Flat Trinity Dissipate chart twice.
Work Rows 17-20 of the Flat Trinity Dissipate chart twice.

Following is a written description of the first 4 rows:
Row 1: Using A2 Sl 1, (Sk2p, 1into3) to M, do not break yarn, SM, lock A2, using C1D1 (Sk2p, 1into3) to last st, K1. 242 sts.
Row 2: Using C1D1 Sl 1, P120, SM, lock C1D1, using A2 P121.
Row 3: Using A2 Sl 1, (1into3, Sk2p) to M, do not break yarn, SM, lock A2, using C1D1 (1into3, Sk2p) to last st, K1.
Row 4: Using C1D1 Sl 1, P120, SM, lock C1D1, using A2 P121.
Rows 5-8: Rep Rows 1-4.
Rows 9-16: Rep Rows 1-8 using A1B1 and D2.
Rows 17-24: Rep Rows 1-8 using B2 and D1E1.
Rows 25-32: Rep Rows 1-8 using B1C1 and E2.
Rows 33-40: Rep Rows 1-8 using C2 and E1F1.
Row 41: Sl 1, P120 sts using C2, SM, lock C2, P121 sts using E1F1.

BO 121 sts in E1F1 using Jeny's Surprisingly Stretchy BO or preferred stretchy BO, then BO the remaining 121 sts using C2.

Finishing

Seam the 2 short ends together using Mattress stitch, or preferred seaming technique, being careful not to twist your work. Weave in ends, wash and block.

Legend:

☐	A2
	A1B1
	B2
	B1C1
■	C2
■	C1D1
	D2
	D1E1
	E2
■	E1F1

knit
knit stitch

sk2p
k2, pass slip st over

(k1 yo k1) in 1 st
k1 leave on needle, yo, then knit again into same st to make 3 sts from 1

slip
RS: slip
WS: slip purlwise with yarn in front

Repeat

Flat Trinity Dissipate Chart

10	9	8	7	6	5	4	3	2	1	
V										20
	λ	∨o	λ	∨o	λ	∨o	λ	∨o	V	19
V										18
	∨o	λ	∨o	λ	∨o	λ	∨o	λ	V	17
V										16
	λ	∨o	λ	∨o	λ	∨o	λ	∨o	V	15
V										14
	∨o	λ	∨o	λ	∨o	λ	∨o	λ	V	13
V										12
	λ	∨o	λ	∨o	λ	∨o	λ	∨o		11
V										10
	∨o	λ	∨o	λ	∨o	λ	∨o	λ	V	9
V										8
	λ	∨o	λ	∨o	λ	∨o	λ	∨o	V	7
V										6
	∨o	λ	∨o	λ	∨o	λ	∨o	λ	V	5
V										4
	λ	∨o	λ	∨o	λ	∨o	λ	∨o	V	3
V										2
	∨o	λ	∨o	λ	∨o	λ	∨o	λ	V	1

Circular Trinity Dissipate Chart

4	3	2	1	
				20
⋏	V°	⋏	V°	19
				18
V°	⋏	V°	⋏	17
				16
⋏	V°	⋏	V°	15
				14
V°	⋏	V°	⋏	13
				12
⋏	V°	⋏	V°	11
				10
V°	⋏	V°	⋏	9
				8
⋏	V°	⋏	V°	7
				6
V°	⋏	V°	⋏	5
				4
⋏	V°	⋏	V°	3
				2
V°	⋏	V°	⋏	1

GRADIENT STRIPED MITTENS

by Carmen Nuland

FINISHED MEASUREMENTS

6 (6.75, 7.25, 8, 8.75)" / 15 (17, 18.5, 20.5, 22) cm circumference x 9.75 (10, 10.5, 11.25, 11.5)" / 25 (25.5, 26.5, 28.5, 29) cm high; to fit Child M, (Women S, Women M, Women L, Men M)

YARN

Knit Picks Wool of the Andes Superwash worsted (100% Superwash Wool; 110 yards/50g): MC Clarity 26337, 1 (1, 2, 2, 2) skein

Knit Picks Chroma Worsted Yarn (70% Superwash Wool, 30% Nylon; 198 yards/100g): C1 Party Hat 26938, 1 skein

NEEDLES

US 5 (3.75mm) DPNs, or two sizes smaller than size to obtain gauge
US 7 (4.5mm) DPNs, or size to obtain gauge

NOTIONS

Yarn Needle
Stitch Markers
Scrap Yarn or Stitch Holder

GAUGE

24 sts and 26 rnds = 4" over stranded stitch pattern in the rnd on larger needles, blocked

Gradient Striped Mittens

Notes:

These mittens look complex but are just a simple two-color stranded design. Using gradient or long-striped yarn for the complimentary color adds another dimension to the pattern.

This pattern is a great starter project for someone who is new to stranded knitting, since the color floats are short.

Read the charts from right to left, knitting all sts.

K2, P2 Ribbing

All Rnds: *K2, P2; rep from * to end of rnd.

Gradient Mitten Stripes Pattern (worked in the rnd over an odd number of sts)

Rnd 1: *With MC K2, with C1 K2; rep from * until 1 st remains; with MC K1.
Rnd 2: MC K1, *C1 K2, MC K2; rep from * to end of rnd.
Rnd 3: *C1 K2, MC K2; rep from * until 1 st remains; C1 K1.
Rnd 4: C1 K1, *MC K2, C1 K2; rep from * to end of rnd.
Rep Rnds 1-4 for pattern.

A tutorial for the Backward Loop CO can be found here: http://tutorials.knitpicks.com/loop-cast-on/

M1L (Make 1 Left-leaning stitch): PU the bar between st just worked and next st and place on LH needle as a regular stitch; K TBL.

M1R (Make 1 Right-leaning stitch): PU the bar between st just worked and next st and place on LH needle backwards (incorrect stitch mount). K through the front loop.

Kitchener Stitch (grafting)

With an equal number of sts on two needles, thread end through yarn needle. Hold needles parallel, with WS's facing in and both needles pointing to the right.

Perform Step 2 on the first front st, and then Step 4 on the first back st, and then continue with instructions below.

1: Pull yarn needle K-wise through front st and drop st from knitting needle.

2: Pull yarn needle P-wise through next front st, leave st on knitting needle.

3: Pull yarn needle P-wise through first back st and drop st from knitting needle.

4: Pull yarn needle K-wise through next back st, leave st on knitting needle.

Rep Steps 1 – 4 until all sts have been grafted.

DIRECTIONS
Cuff

With smaller needles and MC, loosely CO 36 (40, 44, 48, 52) sts. Distribute onto three DPNs, PM and join to work in the rnd, being careful not to twist.

Work in K2, P2 Ribbing for 2.5, (2.5, 2.5, 3, 3)" / (6.5, 6.5, 6.5, 7.5, 7.5) cm, or until cuff is desired length. On last rnd, M1 after last st to create an odd number of sts. 37 (41, 45, 49, 53) sts. Switch to larger needles.

Hand

Work in Gradient Mitten Stripes pattern from line-by-line

instructions or chart, until Hand is 1.5 (1.5, 1.5, 1.75, 1.75)" / 4 (4, 4, 4.5, 4.5) cm above Cuff, ending with Rnd 4.

Thumb Gusset

Rnd 1: PM, C1 M1L, MC K1, MC M1R, PM, MC K1, *C1 K2, MC K2; rep from * until one st remains; MC K1. 2 gusset sts inc, 39 (43, 47, 51, 55) sts.

Rnd 2: SM, MC K2, C1 K1, SM, *C1 K2, MC K2; rep from * to end of rnd.

Rnd 3: SM, C1 M1L, C1 K1, MC K2, C1 M1R, SM, C1 K1, *MC K2, C1 K2; rep from * until three sts remain, MC K2, C1 K1. 2 gusset sts inc, 41 (45, 49, 53, 57) sts.

Rnd 4: SM, C1 K1, MC K2, C1 K2, SM, *MC K2, C1 K2; rep from * to end of rnd.

Rnd 5: SM, C1 M1L, MC K3, C1 K2, MC M1R, SM, MC K1, *C1 K2, MC K2; rep from * until three sts remain, C1 K2, MC K1. 2 gusset sts inc, 43 (47, 51, 55, 59) sts.

Rnd 6: SM, MC K2, C1 K3, MC K2, SM, *C1 K2, MC K2; rep from * to end of rnd.

Rnd 7: SM, C1 M1L, MC K2, C1 K3, MC K2, C1 M1R, SM, C1 K1, *MC K2, C1 K2; rep from * until three sts remain, MC K2, C1 K1. 2 gusset sts inc, 45 (49, 53, 57, 61) sts.

Rnd 8: SM, MC K2, C1 K2, MC K3, C1 K2, SM, *MC K2, C1 K2; rep from * to end of rnd.

6 (6.75, 7.25)" / 15 (17, 18.5) cm Only

Place first 9 gusset sts on stitch holder, removing stitch markers. With MC, CO 1 using Backward Loop CO and rejoin in the round with the CO st as the first st. 37 (41, 45, –, –) sts.

MC K1, *C1 K2, MC K2; rep from * until three sts remain; C1 K2, MC K1.

Beginning with a Rnd 2, work Rnds 1-4 of Gradient Mitten Stripes pattern until mitten is 6.25 (6.5, 7.0, –, –)" / 16 (16.5, 18, –, –) cm in height above the cuff or 1" / (2.5) cm less than desired height. You may end on any rnd.

On the last rnd, K2tog the last two sts. 36 (40, 44, –, –) sts. Continue with Top Decrease.

8 (8.75)" / 20.5 (22) cm Only

Rnd 9: SM, C1 M1L, MC K2, C1 K2, MC K2, C1 K3, MC M1R, SM, MC 1, *C1 K2, MC K2; rep from * until three sts remain, C1 K2, MC K1. – (–, –, 59, 63) sts.

Rnd 10: SM, (MC K2, C1 K2) twice, MC K3, SM, *C1 K2, MC K2; rep from * to end of rnd.

Place first 11 gusset sts on stitch holder, removing stitch markers. With C1, CO 1 using Backward Loop CO and rejoin in the rnd with the CO st as the first st. – (–, –, 49, 53) sts.

C1 K1, *MC K2, C1 K2; rep from * until three sts remain; MC K2, C1 K1.

Beginning with a Rnd 4, work Rnds 1-4 of Gradient Mitten Stripes pattern until mitten is – (–, –, 7.25, 7.5)" / – (–, –, 18.5, 19) cm in height above the cuff or 1" / (2.5) cm less than desired height. You may end on any rnd.

On the last rnd, K2tog the last two sts. – (–, –, 48, 52) sts. Continue with Top Decrease.

All Sizes: There should now be 36 (40, 44, 48, 52) sts on the needles.

Top Decrease

All sizes, use MC only.

Rnd 1: *K1, Ssk, K12 (14, 16, 18, 20), K2tog, K1; rep from * to end of rnd. 32 (36, 40, 44, 48) sts.

Rnd 2: *K1, Ssk, K10 (12, 14, 16, 18), K2tog, K1; rep from * to end of rnd. 28 (32, 36, 40, 44) sts.

Rnd 3: *K1, Ssk, K8 (10, 12, 14, 16), K2tog, K1; rep from * to end of rnd. 24 (28, 32, 36, 40) sts.

Rnd 4: *K1, Ssk, K6 (8, 10, 12, 14), K2tog, K1; rep from * to end of rnd. 20 (24, 28, 32, 36) sts.

Rnd 5: *K1, Ssk, K4 (6, 8, 10, 12), K2tog, K1; rep from * to end of rnd. 16 (20, 24, 28, 32) sts.

Rnd 6 (All Sizes EXCEPT 6" (15 cm): *K1, Ssk, K- (4, 6, 8, 10), K2tog, K1; rep from * to end of rnd. - (16, 20, 24, 28) sts.

Distribute the sts evenly on two needles. Use the Kitchener Stitch to close the top.

Thumb

Move sts from stitch holder to DPNs. Using MC, PU and K 5 (8, 8, 9, 9) sts on opposite side of opening. 14 (17, 17, 20, 20) sts.

Knit around until thumb is at least 1 (1, 1.5, 2, 2)" 2.5 (2.5, 4, 5, 5) cm from start of solid color.

Rnd 1: *K2tog, K1; rep from * until two sts remain, K2tog. 9 (11, 11, 13, 13 sts).

Rnd 2: Knit all sts.

Rnd 3: *K2tog; rep from * until 1 st remains, K1. 5, (6, 6, 7, 7) sts.

Cut a long tail, draw through remaining sts, pull tight and fasten.

Finishing

Weave in ends, wash and block to size.

Legend:

☐	**knit**	knit stitch
◼	MC	
▦ (gray)	C1	
☐	repeat	
▪ (dark)	no stitch	
M̲	**make one left**	Place a firm backward loop over the right needle, so that the yarn end goes towards the front
M̲R	**make one right**	Place a firm backward loop over the right needle, so that the yarn end goes towards the back
│	stitch marker placement	

Graidient Mitten Stripes Chart

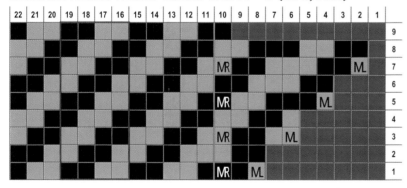

Graidient Mitten Thumb Gusset Chart 1 - 6 (6.75, 7.25)

Gradient Mitten Thumb Gusset Chart 2 - 8 (8.75)

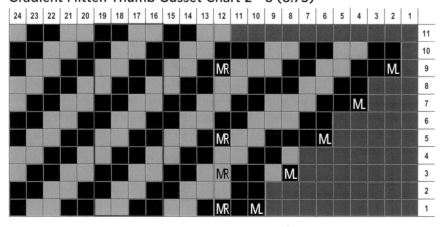

BLUSHING

by Faith Schmidt

FINISHED MEASUREMENTS

7.25 x 106.5"

YARN

Knit Picks Stroll Tonal (75% Superwash
Merino Wool, 25% Nylon; 462 yards/100g): C1
Pearlescent 25385, C2 Seashell 26592, C3 High
Tea 26752, C4 Heartfelt 27079; 1 skein each

NEEDLES

US 9 (5.5mm) straight or circular needles, or
size to obtain gauge

NOTIONS

Yarn Needle

GAUGE

19 sts and 21.5 rows = 4" over Lace Pattern
with yarn held double, lightly blocked. (Gauge
for this project is approximate)

Blushing

Notes:

Starting with a light neutral, and moving to a deep red, Blushing is a fun accessory. Knitting with two strands held together makes this a fairly quick project, and allows the colors to transition more gently. Take your love for gradients to a new level with this long and luscious scarf.

For the purpose of this pattern C1 will be the lightest color, C2 will be the next darkest, and so on through C4. You will always be working with two strands held together.

For a tutorial on the Long Tail Cast On see: http://tutorials.knitpicks.com/long-tail-cast-on/

Lace Pattern (worked flat over a multiple of 16 plus 2 sts)
Row 1 (RS): *P2, K3, K2tog, K1, YO, P2, YO, K1, SSK, K3; rep from * to last 2 sts, P2.
Rows 2, 4, 6, 8 (WS): Purl.
Row 3: *P2, K2, K2tog, K1, YO, K1, P2, K1, YO, K1, SSK, K2; rep from * to last 2 sts, P2.
Row 5: *P2, K1, K2tog, K1, YO, K2, P2, K2, YO, K1, SSK, K1; rep from * to last 2 sts, P2.
Row 7: *P2, K2tog, K1, YO, K3, P2, K3, YO, K1, SSK; rep from * to last 2 sts, P2.
Rep Rows 1-8 for pattern.

DIRECTIONS

With two strands of C1, CO 34 sts using the Long Tail Cast On and knit 1 row.
Work 10 repeats of the Lace Pattern.

Cut one strand of C1 and attach one strand of C2. You will be knitting with two strands of yarn, C1 and C2. Work 10 repeats of the Lace Pattern.

Cut the strand of C1 and attach another strand of C2. You will be knitting with two strands of C2 yarn. Work 10 repeats of the Lace Pattern.

Cut one strand of C2 and attach one strand of C3. You will be knitting with two strands of yarn, C2 and C3. Work 10 repeats of the Lace Pattern.

Cut the strand of C2 and attach another strand of C3. You will be knitting with two strands of C3 yarn. Work 10 repeats of the Lace Pattern.

Cut one strand of C3 and attach one strand of C4. You will be knitting with two strands of yarn, C3 and C4. Work 10 repeats of the Lace Pattern.

Cut the strand of C3 and attach another strand of C4. You will be knitting with two strands of C4 yarn. Work 10 repeats of the Lace Pattern. On the last repeat, end on RS Row 7.

Knit 1 row.
BO loosely, K-wise.

Finishing

Weave in ends, wash and lightly block.

CALAMOSCA COWL

by Sarah Jordan

FINISHED MEASUREMENTS
23.25" outside circumference, 8.5" tall

YARN
Knit Picks Chroma Worsted (70% Superwash Wool, 30% Nylon; 198 yards/100g): C1 Black 25885, C2 Weather Vane 26468; 1 skein each

NEEDLES
US 7 (4.5mm) 24" circular needle, or size to obtain gauge

US 6 (4mm) 24" circular needle, or one size smaller than size to obtain gauge
One spare circular needle in either size

NOTIONS
Yarn Needle
One Stitch Marker
Smooth Waste Yarn (for provisional cast on)

GAUGE
22 sts and 24 rnds = 4" in stranded St st in the rnd on larger needles, blocked

Calamosca Cowl

Notes:

This cowl is even warmer than a typical stranded piece because it has an inner and an outer layer, effectively giving you four layers of fabric when complete. All the floats will be hidden inside the layers of fabric when complete, so while you may wish to catch some of the longer floats to help keep your tension even, there is no need to do so out of concern that they might get caught on something. It is worked as one long tube, which is then folded in half when the two ends are connected.

Color dominance is something to keep in mind when knitting this pattern. When you're working with more than one color, the path each strand takes can have an effect on the visual outcome. In stranded colorwork, typically the yarn that comes from underneath will "pop" more in the design. In this cowl, the color you use for C2 should be the strand that comes from underneath.

When working the charts, follow each row from right to left, as a RS row.

Three-Needle Bind Off

Hold needles parallel so that the sts forming the outside of the cowl are on the needle held to the front and the sts forming the inside of the cowl are to the back. Using the spare needle as the right needle, insert the tip as if to knit through the first stitch on the front needle and then as if to knit through the first stitch on the back needle. Wrap the yarn around the right needle tip and pull the resulting loop through both sts, then pull the sts off the left needles. *Work another st the same way, inserting the right needle through one st on both needles held in the left hand. Using the tip of one of the needles held in the left hand, pull the first st on the right needle over the second st and off the needle. Rep from * until all sts have been bound off.

DIRECTIONS

Using waste yarn and a provisional method of your choice, CO 128 sts. With C1 and larger needles, K across all provisionally CO sts, then join in the rnd, being careful not to twist, and PM to indicate beginning of rnd.

Outside of Cowl

K four rnds in C1.

Join C2 and work the colorwork pattern shown in Chart A; each line of the chart is worked eight times per rnd. Work Rnds 1-6 of Chart A seven times.

K four rnds in C1.

Next Rnd (Turning Rnd): P in C1.

Inside of Cowl

Switch to smaller needles and K one rnd in C1, then K three rnds in C2.

Work the colorwork pattern shown in Chart B; each line of the chart is worked 64 times per rnd. Work Rnds 1 and 2 of Chart B twenty-one times.

K three rnds in C2. Break C2, leaving a tail to weave in later.

K one rnd in C1.

Before proceeding, weave in all ends and trim yarn tails.

Undo provisional CO and place live sts on larger needle. Pull Chart B section of cowl inside Chart A section, folding at the P Turning Rnd and aligning sts on needles. With spare needle, do a Three-Needle Bind Off to connect the two sets of sts and close cowl. When all sts have been bound off, cut C1 and pull tail through final st.

Finishing

Weave in final end and trim yarn tail. Block as desired.

Chart A

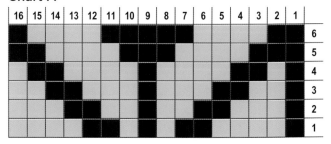

Chart B

Legend:

□ **knit**
knit stitch

■ C1

▨ C2

TALIA CAFÉ BAG

by illitilli

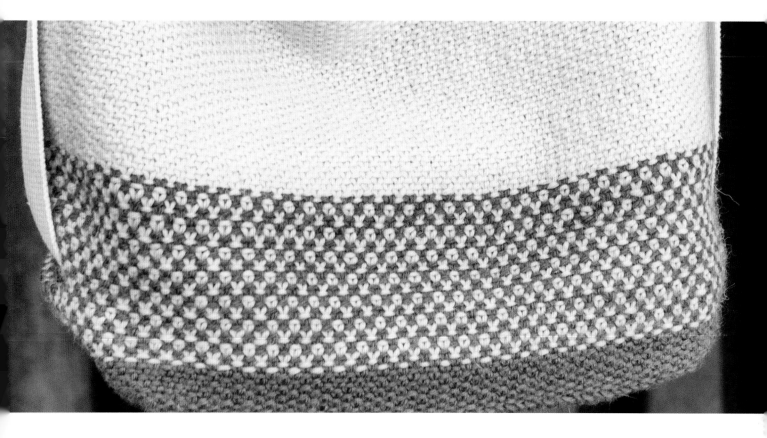

FINISHED MEASUREMENTS

9.5" wide x 4" deep at base; 9.5" high

YARN

Knit Picks Wool of the Andes Superwash Worsted (100% Superwash Wool; 110 yards/50g): MC Clarity 26337, 2 balls; C1 Cadet 26339, 1 ball

NEEDLES

US 6 (4mm) 32" or longer circular needle, or size to obtain gauge

US 6 (4mm) DPNs, or size to obtain gauge, set of 3

US 3 (3.25mm) needle for I-cord, or three sizes smaller than size to obtain gauge

NOTIONS

Lining Fabric, 2 pieces: approximately 14"x 25" and 8.5" x 10"

Light Weight Fusible Interfacing, 2 pieces, approximately 13.5"x 9.5" each

Plastic Mesh, approximately 4" x 9. 5"

Strap: Raw cut leather strapping or cotton webbing, 1.75" wide x approximately 60"; Leather Needles and Waxed Thread; Awl

Sewing Needle and Thread

Magnetic Snap, 0.5" diameter

Yarn Needle

Stitch Markers

Scrap Yarn

Corrugated Cardboard, approximately 12"x 25"

Packing Tape or Plastic Wrap

Iron

Sewing Machine (optional)

GAUGE

26 sts and 47 rows = 4" in Fabric Stitch on larger needles, blocked

Talia Café Bag

Notes:

Worked in a very dense fabric, this bag will hold its shape and withstand plenty of use.

Starting with a provisional cast on, the base of the bag is worked flat. Stitches are then picked up along the sides and joined with the live and provisionally cast on stitches to work the remainder of the bag in the round. One Row Buttonholes are incorporated into the bottom and sides of the bag to secure the strap.

YB (Yarn Back): Move yarn to back of work.

Make Buttonhole (One Row Buttonhole)

SL1 WYIF, YB, *(SL1, PSSO) 13x, SL last st worked back to left needle, turn. Reverse Cable CO 13 sts, turn.

Reverse Cable Cast On

Insert right needle between 1st and 2nd sts on left needle from the back of the work, wrap with working yarn as if to purl, pull through a loop to the back and place on left needle.

Fabric Stitch (worked in the round over an odd number of sts)

Rnd 1: (K1, SL1 WYIF) to last st, K1.
Rnd 2: (SL1 WYIF, K1) to last st, SL1 WYIF.
Rep Rnds 1-2 for pattern.

DIRECTIONS

Bag Bottom

Using larger needles and scrap yarn, provisionally CO 29 sts.
Row 1 (WS): Join C1 and Purl.
Row 2 (RS): SL1 K-wise, (K1, SL1 WYIF) to last 2 sts, K2.
Row 3: SL1, (SL1 WYIB, P1) to end.
Rows 2 and 3 form the basic pattern rows for the bag bottom.
Rows 4-7: Cont in pattern.
Row 8: SL1 K-wise, (K1, SL1 WYIF) 3x, K1, Make Buttonhole, (K1, SL1 WYIF) to last 2 sts, K2.
Rows 9-17: Cont in pattern.
Row 18: Rep Row 8.
Cont in pattern until work measures 6.5" from buttonhole Row 18, ending after a WS row. Rep Rows 8 through 18, work 7 more rows in pattern, then proceed to Bag Body.

Bag Body

Pick Up Sts for Working in the Round

Step 1: With RS facing and using a DPN, SL1 K-wise, (K1, SL1 WYIF) to end.

Step 2: Turn work 90 degrees. Using a circular needle, PU and K TBL the RS leg of each slipped st. This must be an ODD number of sts to maintain the fabric stitch pattern – skip picking up the first st if you have an even number of slipped sts.

Step 3: PM2 for bag corner. Turn work 90 degrees. Remove scrap yarn from provisional CO and place sts on a DPN. Using a second DPN, (SL1 WYIF, K1) to last st, SL1 WYIF.

Step 4: Turn work 90 degrees. Using the working end of your circular needle, PU and K TBL the RS leg of each slipped st from the remaining side of the rectangular bag bottom. This must be an EVEN number of sts to maintain the fabric stitch pattern – skip picking up the first st if you have an odd number of slipped sts. PM1 for start of rnd.

Step 5: Work in Fabric Stitch until bag body measures 1" from picked up sts, ending after Rnd 1 of the stitch pattern. DPNs may be removed once there is enough ease at the bag corners to work in the round with your 32" circular.

Color Transition Band

Rnd 1: (SL1 WYIF, K1) 4x, Make Buttonhole, (K1, SL1 WYIF) to last st before M2, K1, SM, (SL1 WYIF, K1) 4x, Make Buttonhole, (K1, SL1 WYIF) to end.
Rnds 2-3: Join MC. Work Fabric Stitch using MC.
Rnds 4-5: Work in pattern using C1.
Rnds 6-7: Work in pattern using MC.
Rnds 8-9: Work in pattern using C1.
Rnd 10: Work in pattern using MC.
Rnd 11: Repeat Rnd 1 using MC.

Cont in pattern, alternating two rnds of C1 with two rnds of MC until the color transition band measures 2.5" or you run out of C1, making sure to finish after a complete rnd of C1. Cont in pattern in MC until work measures 8" from the picked up sts on the bag bottom, then rep Rnd 1. Work 9 rnds in pattern, then repeat Rnd 1 again. Work 6 more rnds in pattern, then proceed to I-cord BO.

I-cord BO

Cable CO 2 sts with MC.
Using smaller needle for the right needle, *K1, SL1, K1, PSSO, SL 2 worked sts back to left needle; rep from * to last 2 sts.
Break MC, leaving a tail of 12". Graft the 2 live sts to the 2 CO sts to complete the I-cord BO.

Finishing

Weave in ends.

Blocking

Create a blocking form by cutting, scoring, folding and taping a piece of corrugated cardboard as shown in Diagram A, adjusting the form size as required to suit your bag. To prevent the cardboard form from losing its shape while blocking, wrap it completely in packing tape or plastic wrap. Wet block the bag on the form, propping the form upside down until the fabric is dry.

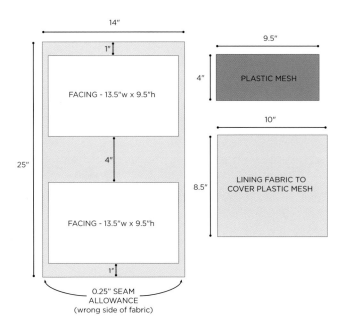

Construct Lining

Measure and cut lining fabric, fusible facing and plastic mesh as shown in Diagram B, adjusting the lining and facing sizes to suit your blocked knitting. You may find it useful to cut and assemble a paper template of the lining to test for fit. Using a hot, dry iron, fuse the facings to the wrong side of your lining fabric as shown.

Fold the lining in half and sew the side seams using a sewing needle and thread and a running stitch, or sewing machine. Clip the tip of the seam allowance at the corner points as shown in Diagram C and press the seams open. Sew across the points at each end of the bottom, fold up the resulting triangular flap, and tack the flap to the side seams (see Diagram D), this forms the squared ends of the lining bottom. Fold the unfaced 1" of fabric along the top of the bag to the outside and press.

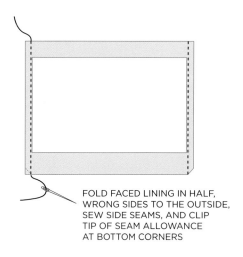

FOLD FACED LINING IN HALF, WRONG SIDES TO THE OUTSIDE, SEW SIDE SEAMS, AND CLIP TIP OF SEAM ALLOWANCE AT BOTTOM CORNERS

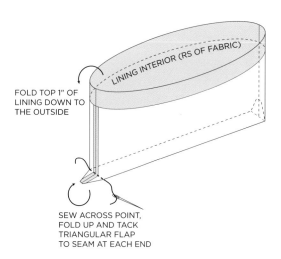

FOLD TOP 1" OF LINING DOWN TO THE OUTSIDE

SEW ACROSS POINT, FOLD UP AND TACK TRIANGULAR FLAP TO SEAM AT EACH END

Fold the fabric to cover the base stiffener in half, RS's together, and sew the side and bottom seams. Turn right side out, press, insert plastic mesh, fold top seam to the inside and sew closed with a whip stitch. Insert the base stiffener into the bottom of the lining and pin in place. Use a whip stitch on the wrong side of the lining fabric to secure the base stiffener inside the lining.

Magnetic Snap

Attach one half of the magnetic snap to each side of the lining opening at the center points of the long sides, approximately 1" down from the top edge.

Attach Lining

Insert the lining into the knitted bag, aligning the lining base with the bag bottom, and the top edge of the lining with the underside of the I-cord BO. Check to make sure the lining seams do not show on the outside of the bag, and if necessary, tack and/or trim the seam allowances to achieve a smooth finish. Pin the lining in place. Using a sewing needle and thread and a whip stitch, sew the upper edge of the lining to the underside of the I-cord on the bag interior.

Attach Strap

Insert one end of the strap down through the buttonhole slots on each side the bag, around and through to the bottom center. For cotton webbing, overlap strap ends by 1.5" and sew together as shown in Diagram E, by hand or machine using heavy thread. For raw cut leather strapping, overlap strap ends by 1.5", mark stitch points and pierce with a stitching awl before sewing by hand using leather needles and waxed thread, and the Two Needle method.

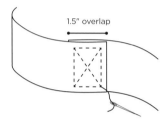

1.5" overlap

Abbreviations

BO	bind off	M	marker		stitch	TBL	through back loop
cn	cable needle	M1	make one stitch	RH	right hand	TFL	through front loop
CC	contrast color	M1L	make one left-leaning	rnd(s)	round(s)	tog	together
CDD	Centered double dec		stitch	RS	right side	W&T	wrap & turn (see
CO	cast on	M1R	make one right-lean-	Sk	skip		specific instructions
cont	continue		ing stitch	Sk2p	sl 1, k2tog, pass		in pattern)
dec	decrease(es)	MC	main color		slipped stitch over	WE	work even
DPN(s)	double pointed	P	purl		k2tog: 2 sts dec	WS	wrong side
	needle(s)	P2tog	purl 2 sts together	SKP	sl, k, psso: 1 st dec	WYIB	with yarn in back
EOR	every other row	PM	place marker	SL	slip	WYIF	with yarn in front
inc	increase	PFB	purl into the front and	SM	slip marker	YO	yarn over
K	knit		back of stitch	SSK	sl, sl, k these 2 sts tog		
K2tog	knit two sts together	PSSO	pass slipped stitch	SSP	sl, sl, p these 2 sts tog		
KFB	knit into the front and		over		tbl		
	back of stitch	PU	pick up	SSSK	sl, sl, sl, k these 3 sts		
K-wise	knitwise	P-wise	purlwise		tog		
LH	left hand	rep	repeat	St st	stockinette stitch		
		Rev St st	reverse stockinette	sts	stitch(es)		

Knit Picks yarn is both luxe and affordable—a seeming contradiction trounced! But it's not just about the pretty colors; we also care deeply about fiber quality and fair labor practices, leaving you with a gorgeously reliable product you'll turn to time and time again.

THIS COLLECTION FEATURES

Chroma Worsted
Worsted Weight
70% Superwash, 30% Nylon

Chroma Fingering
Fingering Weight
70% Superwash, 30% Nylon

Stroll Gradient
Fingering Weight
75% Superwash Merino Wool,
25% Nylon

Stroll Tonal
Fingering Weight
75% Superwash Merino Wool,
25% Nylon

Brava Worsted
Worsted Weight
100% Premium Acrylic

Swish Worsted
Worsted Weight
100% Superwash Merino Wool

Alpaca Cloud
Fingering
& Lace Weight
100% Baby Alpaca

Chroma Twist Fingering
Fingering Weight
70% Superwash, 30% Nylon

Chroma Twist Bulky
Bulky Weight
70% Superwash, 30% Nylon

View these beautiful yarns and more at www.KnitPicks.com